DESTINY'S ARCHITECT

CRAFTING YOUR PATH TO MASTERY

HONEY SHARMA

Made with ♥ on the Notion Press Platform
www.notionpress.com

This book is dedicated to my friends, family, and loving daughter Deetya. Thank you for being my support and teacher throughout my life.

Contents

Preface

In every person's life, there is a special power—the power to make things happen through our thoughts. This power goes beyond the ordinary and encourages us to discover the amazing potential of our minds.

Welcome to the beginning of a life-changing journey, where we explore the mind and the incredible skill of turning thoughts into reality.

As the author, I invite you to join me on this journey to understand how our minds can shape the world around us.

This journey is more than just wishful thinking or saying positive words. It is a deep exploration of how the mind can turn our dreams and desires into reality.

In the next pages, you will find ideas, techniques, and wisdom from both ancient traditions and modern psychology.

Through manifestation, we will uncover the mind's secrets, understand its power, and learn how to use it to create a life that truly reflects our deepest dreams.

This book does not promise instant miracles or a single solution for everyone. Instead, it is a guide to help you understand and use the natural power of your mind.

As we explore manifestation, we will learn different techniques, practice exercises, and see real-life examples of how focused thoughts and belief can bring great changes.

This journey begins by understanding the basic principles of manifestation. We will explore how our thoughts, emotions, and energy work together to shape our reality.

You will find practical exercises to help you focus your mind on your desires, develop a positive mindset, and remove obstacles that may block your progress.

Inside these pages, you will read stories of people who used the power of their minds to create incredible changes in their lives. Their experiences show that manifestation is not just for a few—it is a gift available to anyone who is ready to use it.

As we go on this journey together, I hope you will discover the amazing abilities of your mind and learn how to use these ideas in your daily life.

May this book be your guide, giving you support and motivation as you unlock your inner power.

So, dear reader, let's begin. Free your mind, embrace manifestation, and create the life you truly want.

With anticipation,

Honey Sharma

Prologue

When I was in college, I found an MLM company. Their smart-talking employees convinced me, a simple student, to invest my money and join their team.

I joined right away and went to their training sessions, even though a lot of it was hard to understand.

I was full of motivation and believed I could do anything. I dreamed of big cars, huge houses, and a fancy life—even though I hadn't made any money yet.

I was blindly inspired, not knowing how hard real life can be. Then one day, my trainer told us an interesting story about gods and powerful energy.

The Story of the Gods

In a meeting of gods, they decided to create a great power that could change the world—something unbelievable but very strong.

With great wisdom and energy, the gods combined heavenly forces to create a power beyond human understanding.

"A divine assembly shaping the power to transform the world."

This power could awaken hidden abilities, helping people achieve greatness and endless possibilities. It was inside every person, waiting to be unlocked by belief.

But the gods' success did not last long. The bright, powerful energy attracted everyone who saw it. The gods tried to hide it deep in the ocean and even in space, but humans, being clever, still found a way to reach it.

Worried and unsure of what to do, the gods decided on a new plan—**they placed the power inside humans.**

"The gods' final gift—divine power entrusted to humanity."

Just like Thor's hammer, **only those who could find this hidden power inside themselves would have the ability to achieve anything.**

I had no idea that this story would become part of my own life. Nothing special changed for me. I finished college and got a job in the BPO industry, but I wasn't happy with it.

One day, while cleaning up files on my laptop, I found an old video called **"The Secret."**

It brought back memories of the MLM company—my senior had uploaded this video years ago.

With nothing else to do on a Sunday, I decided to watch it. In just 1.5 hours, I was shocked to learn that thoughts alone could make amazing things happen.

"A forgotten video, a new realization—the power of thought unfolds."

Feeling curious and excited, I started learning more and trying out the ideas from the movie. To my surprise, the things I imagined started to happen in real life.

In this book, I will share my personal experiences and how **The Secret** has completely changed my life.

Understanding the Universe

The universe is huge, full of galaxies, solar systems, planets, and life on Earth. Just like that, our bodies are made of many complex parts, from bones and muscles to tiny atoms and even smaller particles.

Science may use big words, but the idea is simple—everything, whether visible or invisible, has energy. This includes things like paper, pens, money, and even people.

We are also energy beings, carrying the powerful energy that the gods once gave us.

The Energy Connection

At the tiniest level, everything—both living and non-living—is linked in a huge energy field. You don't need to understand difficult science; just know that the energy inside and around us is very powerful.

Come along on this journey to discover this energy and learn how to use it.

By following the ideas in this book, you can attract wonderful things into your life and achieve what once felt impossible.

Let's begin!

CHAPTER ONE

INTERCONNECTED COSMOS

The Universe and Our Connection

The universe is huge and full of mysteries that have amazed people for centuries. When we look at the night sky, the endless stars and planets remind us of how big and wonderful the cosmos is.

Our goal is to explore these mysteries and understand how the universe, divine forces, and humanity are connected, as mentioned in ancient texts.

By looking at science, philosophy, and religious teachings, we try to understand our place in the universe and the deep link we share with it.

This journey is not just about science or spirituality—it touches every part of our lives.

Ancient scriptures from both the East and the West share an important truth—we **are not separate beings but connected parts of something much bigger.**

"Embracing the universe—where science meets spirituality"

Christopher Morley once said-*"In every man's heart, there is a secret nerve that answers to the vibrations of beauty."*

By accepting both science and spirituality, we can better understand our place in the universe. This idea matches ancient wisdom, which teaches that everything is connected.

This journey helps us see the balance between science and spirituality, revealing the beautiful harmony of life within the grand plan of the universe.

The Journey of Two Friends

Aryan and Raj grew up in a small, peaceful village surrounded by green hills and big forests. Their days were full of fun, laughter, and adventure. They ran through narrow paths, climbed tall trees, and explored hidden caves, turning everything around them into a magical playground.

"Two young souls, bound by adventure and laughter."

Every morning brought a new adventure—fishing in the river, chasing fireflies at night, or listening to the village elders tell old, fascinating stories. Their friendship grew stronger with every secret they shared and every dream they whispered, making their bond unbreakable.

As time passed, their adventures changed. They built wooden rafts, dared each other to cross a shaky old bridge that people said was haunted, and found joy in simple things—skipping stones, carving their names into trees, and eating stolen mangoes on warm afternoons.

The village, with its soft winds and wise old trees, was their first teacher. It taught them to love nature and believe in the mysteries of life. But they had no idea that these fun-filled days were preparing them for a journey bigger than they had ever imagined.

As they grew older, life became confusing. They had work, money, and comfort, yet something felt missing. One evening, as they sat under a big banyan tree, Raj said, "Aryan, do you ever wonder why we are here? What is the real meaning of life?"

Aryan nodded and said, "Yes, Raj. We have everything we need, yet something still feels missing. Maybe it's time to find the answers."

Wanting guidance, they spoke to Aryan's father. Listening to their thoughts, he smiled and said, "If you seek wisdom, travel to the ancient temple in the mountains. The monks there have spent their lives understanding the meaning of life."

Inspired by his words, Aryan and Raj embarked on their journey, hoping to discover the truth that had always seemed distant.

Drawn to the Sacred

After days of walking through forests and crossing rivers, they finally reached the temple. The grand entrance stood tall, its ancient stone walls covered in carvings that told stories of wisdom and time.

A soft breeze carried the scent of incense, and the distant sound of monks chanting created a peaceful atmosphere. Birds fluttered near the temple bells as if welcoming travelers to this sacred place.

With a deep breath, they walked inside, ready to begin the journey that could change their lives forever. The air was filled with the sweet smell of incense, and the monks' deep chants echoed through the temple, touching something inside their hearts.

A kind old monk welcomed them. "What brings you here, my children?" he asked with a gentle smile.

"We are searching for the real meaning of life," Raj said. "Can you help us understand?"

The monk nodded. "Stay here for some time. Observe, listen, and you will find your answers."

For days, Aryan and Raj watched the monks praying. They woke up before sunrise, prayed, worked in the garden, helped the poor, and smiled as if they had no worries.

Every prayer they did felt like a link between people and a higher power, connecting them to something bigger than themselves. In the soft light of oil lamps, they saw their journey—doubts, hope, and the search for wisdom.

The holy books they read spoke about balance in the universe, how actions have consequences and the incredible power inside every person. Each lesson they learned made them understand more, helping them see that they were part of something much bigger.

With each day, the confusion in their minds faded, and they felt closer to finding the truth within themselves. The temple songs stayed in their hearts, guiding them beyond simple thinking and into a deep understanding of life.

One day, Aryan asked a monk, "Why do you live this simple life? Don't you want riches and success?"

The monk smiled. *"True success is not in gold or fame. It is in peace. You will find true happiness when you stop running after things and start looking inside yourself."*

Raj asked another monk, "How can we find our purpose?"

The monk replied, *"Purpose is not found outside. It is within you. Do what makes your heart feel full. Help others, spread kindness, and live with love. That is the true meaning of life."*

The sage's words resonated deeply with them. He explained that every thought, action, and emotion contributed to this cosmic dance, shaping their reality.

"The universe is not separate from you," he said. "It flows through you, just as you flow through it. To understand this is to unlock the power within."

Their doubts were gone, and their minds became clear—like the universe had shared its hidden secrets with them. They stepped out of the temple with happy hearts and bright spirits, carrying its wisdom with them forever.

The Essence of Prayer and Intuition

He explained that prayer was not just a ritual but a powerful energy exchange—an alignment of one's intentions with the universal flow.

"When you pray," the sage said, "you are not merely asking; you are attuning yourself to the vibrations of the cosmos. True prayer is a state of being, a harmony between thought, emotion, and belief."

He paused and continued, "Most people think prayer is about words, but it is more about feeling. The universe does not respond to language; it responds to the energy behind it. When your heart and mind unite in faith, you create a bridge between the seen and the unseen. And in that sacred space, miracles unfold effortlessly."

It quietly guides us, helping us sense things beyond logic and reason. When we learn to trust it, we unlock a deep connection with the universe, allowing us to make choices that align with our true path.

"It is a silent guide," he said, "a deep knowing that connects you to the cosmic flow. Trust it, and it will lead you to clarity and purpose."

He then added, "Intuition speaks in whispers, never in shouts. It nudges you gently, often disguised as a feeling or a sudden insight. The more you honor it, the stronger it becomes. Those who listen to their inner voice walk a path of wisdom, free from doubt and fear."

"The sage reveals the universe within and beyond."

Discovering Hidden Powers

As Aryan and Raj sat under the big, starry sky, they felt a special energy flowing through them, as if they were becoming one with the universe.

By staying calm and focusing their minds, they learned to listen to their inner voice. This new understanding changed the way they saw the world, helping them realize how deeply connected they were to everything around them.

A Divine Realization

While meditating deeply, Aryan and Raj had a powerful vision. The universe no longer felt like a space—it was alive, full of energy.

They saw the stars beating like hearts and the planets drifting like thoughts in a vast, endless mind.

In that moment, they understood that everything was connected, woven together in a never-ending flow of energy and awareness.

"The more I know, the more I realize I don't know." - Albert Einstein

The gods were not distant beings in the sky. Instead, they were part of the universe's energy, present in everything.

Aryan and Raj realized that divinity was not just in temples or holy books—it was in every breath, every star, and every moment. The universe was alive, always speaking to those who were ready to listen.

They felt an unshakable truth settle within them: the answers they sought were never outside—they had always been within.

With eyes wide open and hearts full of wonder, they knew they had touched something eternal, something beyond words yet closer than their soul.

Transformation and Return

After their journey, Aryan and Raj returned to their village, filled with new wisdom. Their faces glowed with understanding, and they were eager to share what they had learned. They helped others see the power of the universe and the strength within themselves. Soon, people started coming to them for guidance, seeking answers about life and spirituality.

Through meditation, stories, and old traditions, Aryan and Raj helped others discover their true potential, inspiring them to believe in their inner power. Even though they had traveled far, they knew their greatest purpose was here—to light the way for those ready to find their strength and wisdom.

Their story spread across India, becoming a well-known legend.

Discovering the Universe

As time passed, Aryan and Raj kept exploring the universe inside and around them. They realized their journey had no end. It was a continuous dance with the energies that shape life. They understood that the universe was not far away—it lived within every heartbeat and breath.

The story of Aryan and Raj became a legend, carried by the wind and echoed by the rivers. The universe kept revealing its secrets to those who listened, showing how all living beings are connected in the grand design of existence.

"The cosmos is within us. We are made of star stuff. We are a way for the universe to know itself." – Carl Sagan

Thinking About Our Connection

As we reflect on their journey, we wonder:

- Are we connected to the universe?
- Could the energy inside us be linked to the cosmos, proving we are all part of something bigger?
- Is our consciousness merely an individual experience, or is it woven into the fabric of existence?

- Do our thoughts and emotions ripple through the universe, shaping the reality around us?
- If everything is interconnected, can we harness this energy to influence our destiny?
- Could ancient wisdom and modern science both be revealing the same truth in different ways?

Imagine how everything in the world—both living and non-living—is connected, always influencing each other like a beautiful dance in the universe.

The trees give us oxygen, and we give them carbon dioxide. The sun gives light, helping plants grow, which then provides food for animals and humans. Even the smallest breeze can create ripples in a pond, just as a kind word can brighten someone's day.

Every action creates a reaction, shaping the world around us in ways we may not always see. The universe is not just a collection of separate things—it is one big, flowing system where everything plays a role.

When we understand this deep connection, we realize that our thoughts, actions, and energy also shape the world. By living with kindness and awareness, we become part of this great cosmic balance, adding harmony to the dance of life.

The Power of Prayer and Thought

Our thoughts and prayers may act like invisible signals, aligning with the universe's energy. When we focus our minds, we might be connecting to something beyond what we can see. Just like radio waves travel through the air without being visible, our intentions and emotions may send out unseen vibrations that shape our reality.

Many believe that positive thoughts attract positive outcomes, like a magnet pulling things toward it. When we truly believe in something, we may unknowingly guide events in that direction. In the same way, prayers and deep desires might reach the universe, bringing back answers in unexpected ways.

Perhaps the universe listens, not just to our words, but to the energy behind them, responding in ways that align with our deepest hopes and intentions.

"Prayer aligns the soul with the universe's energy."

Prayer helps us connect with the universe's energy. It allows us to seek guidance, find comfort, and express gratitude. When we pray with true belief, it calms our minds and fills our hearts with hope. It reminds us that we are not alone and that there is a greater force always listening.

Through prayer, we release our worries and open ourselves to new possibilities. It strengthens our faith, helping us trust the journey even when we don't see the full path ahead. Whether whispered in silence or spoken aloud, every sincere prayer carries energy, creating ripples that may bring peace, healing, and answers in ways we least expect.

The Power of Thoughts

Our thoughts and feelings can shape our lives, just like the law of attraction says. Whatever we focus on brings similar energy into our world. Can the energy inside us help make our dreams come true? The way our thoughts and the universe connect is an interesting idea to think about.

Every thought has energy. When we think positive things, we attract good things into our lives. Just like a tiny seed grows into a big tree with time and care, our dreams can also come true if we believe in them and work toward them.

If we fill our minds with fear and doubt, it can stop good things from coming. But if we have faith and stay strong, we can make things happen. Our thoughts are powerful. Maybe the universe is like a mirror, giving back whatever energy we send out. If we think with hope, gratitude, and confidence, we open the way for wonderful things to come into our lives.

Discovering Life's Secrets

As we think about how we are connected to everything, the power of prayer, and the strength of our thoughts, our journey of understanding continues.

"The most beautiful thing we can experience is the mysterious. It is the source of all true art and science." - Albert Einstein

We will explore these ideas even more, discovering how being in tune with the universe's energy can lead to success and happiness in life.

Until then, move through each day with awareness. Pay attention to the little things around you, as they often hold deep meaning.

Notice how your thoughts shape your experiences and how the energy you give out comes back to you. The world is full of signs and lessons, waiting for those who take the time to see them.

Be open to learning, trust the journey, and remember that life always has more wisdom to share with those who listen. Every moment, every experience, and every thought is a part of something bigger.

CHAPTER TWO

THE ALCHEMY OF CONSCIOUS AND SUBCONSCIOUS MINDS

The human mind is very powerful and complex. It controls our thoughts, feelings, actions, and how we see the world. Every choice we make, every habit we form, and every belief we have comes from the mind.

Experts have studied the mind for a long time and found that it has two main parts: the conscious mind and the subconscious mind. Each part has its role in how we understand things, respond to situations, and live our lives.

The conscious mind helps us think, analyze, and make decisions, while the subconscious mind stores memories, habits, and emotions that shape our actions.

By understanding how these two parts work together, we can improve our thoughts, change negative patterns, and create a better future for ourselves.

Understanding the Conscious Mind

The conscious mind is the part of our brain that controls our thoughts, feelings, and what we are aware of in the present moment. It helps us think, make decisions, and solve problems.

Because of this awareness, we can reflect on our past, set goals, and make choices on purpose. The conscious mind also acts like a filter, taking in information from the world around us while being influenced by our deeper subconscious mind.

Key Characteristics of the Conscious Mind:

Awareness and Attention:

The conscious mind is all about awareness and focus. It helps us pay attention to certain thoughts and use our mental energy for important tasks or goals.

Our awareness affects how we see life, shaping our feelings, thoughts, and the way we interact with the world. When we become more aware, we can control how we respond to situations instead of reacting without thinking.

Choice and Purpose

Volition means using our willpower to make decisions that shape our lives. It allows us to choose our actions on purpose. The conscious mind helps us set goals, make plans, and take meaningful steps toward our future.

When we act with purpose, we give meaning to our actions, making sure they match our values and dreams.

Thinking and Decision-Making

The conscious mind helps us think carefully, analyze information, and make smart choices. It allows us to understand situations, solve problems, and use logic to make good decisions.

When we think deeply, we can break big problems into smaller parts, consider different ideas, and find the best solutions.

Short-term Memory:

Short-term memory is a part of the conscious mind that helps us remember small bits of information for a short time, like a phone number or a set of directions. It acts like a temporary storage system, keeping important details available when we need them for quick thinking and decision-making.

However, short-term memory has limited capacity and can only hold information for a few seconds to a minute. If we don't repeat or use the information, it quickly fades away.

To make short-term memory stronger, we can practice mental exercises like solving puzzles, meditating, and repeating important details. These activities help train the brain to store and recall information better.

Science Connection: Studies show that the brain can hold around 7 pieces of information in short-term memory at once, which is why phone numbers are often 7 digits long.

Mythology Link: In Greek mythology, the River Lethe was said to erase memories of the past, similar to how the brain forgets unused information. Just like souls in Greek myths had to drink from the river to forget, our minds also need practice to keep memories alive.

Understanding the Subconscious Mind

The conscious mind is like the small visible part of an iceberg, handling logic, reasoning, and daily decisions. But beneath the surface, the subconscious mind works like a giant unseen force, shaping our thoughts, emotions, and actions without us even realizing it.

It works in the background, constantly taking in and storing information from our surroundings. Even when we are not paying attention, our subconscious absorbs everything we see, hear, and feel.

This part of the mind holds a huge collection of memories, experiences, and automatic habits. It shapes how we react to situations, what we believe, and how we feel about things.

Science Connection: Neuroscientists believe that about 95% of our daily actions come from the subconscious mind. This is why we can do things like drive a car or walk without thinking too much—it becomes automatic.

Mythology Link: In Hindu mythology, the Chitta, a part of the mind, is often compared to a deep ocean that holds all past experiences, emotions, and desires. Like the subconscious, it silently influences a person's actions and destiny, shaping their life based on past impressions (samskaras).

By understanding and training the subconscious mind, we can change old habits, overcome fears, and create a better future for ourselves.

Key Characteristics of the Subconscious Mind

i) **Automatic Processes:** The subconscious mind controls many automatic functions like heartbeat, breathing, and learned behaviors, making our daily actions more efficient.

ii) **Long-Term Memory:** It stores memories, experiences, and learned associations that may not always be in our immediate awareness.

iii) **Emotional Responses:** It shapes our emotions by storing past emotional experiences, influencing how we react to different situations.

iv) **Habitual Behavior:** It manages routines and habits, allowing us to perform tasks automatically without thinking too much.

v) **Intuition and Gut Feelings:** The subconscious mind often guides us through instincts or gut feelings, helping in quick decision-making without conscious reasoning.

vi) Protective Mechanism: It acts as a defense system by suppressing painful memories or traumatic experiences to protect our mental well-being.

Connection Between the Conscious and Subconscious Mind

Both parts of the mind—the conscious mind and the subconscious mind—are always working together, shaping our thoughts, feelings, and actions. The conscious mind helps us think, analyze situations, and make choices in the present moment. It is the part we use when we focus, solve problems, or learn something new.

The subconscious mind, on the other hand, works quietly in the background. It stores memories, past experiences, and automatic habits, influencing how we react to things without us even realizing it.

For example, when you ride a bicycle, your conscious mind helps you learn, but after practice, the subconscious takes over, allowing you to cycle without thinking about every movement.

The brain processes millions of pieces of information every second, but we are only aware of a small part of it. This is why the subconscious handles many tasks automatically. This shows how both must work together for a balanced life.

How They Work Together

Processing Information:
The subconscious mind works like a supercomputer, quickly handling large amounts of information every second. It sorts, organizes, and filters everything we see,

hear, and feel, keeping only the most important details and sending them to the conscious mind.

This helps us focus on tasks without getting distracted by every little sound, sight, or movement around us. For example, when walking through a crowded street, the subconscious blocks out unnecessary background noise so we can pay attention to crossing the road or recognizing a friend in the crowd.

The subconscious also helps us do everyday tasks automatically. Once we learn a skill like typing, cycling, or driving, we no longer have to think about every movement—the subconscious takes over and does it for us.

It also helps us recognize patterns in faces, places, or emotions. This is why we quickly notice someone we know, even in a big crowd, or sense when a situation feels familiar. Even when we are not aware of it, our subconscious keeps working, shaping our thoughts, emotions, and decisions in ways we don't always realize.

Scientists say the subconscious mind can process 11 million bits of information per second, while the conscious mind can only handle about 40 bits. This shows how much work happens behind the scenes in our minds.

Beliefs and Attitudes:

Over time, the thoughts we repeat, the things we learn from society, and our personal experiences become deeply stored in our subconscious. This is why some beliefs become so strong that they guide our actions without us even thinking about them.

Many of these beliefs start forming in childhood, influenced by parents, teachers, and society. The way we see ourselves, how we handle relationships, and even our ability to succeed are shaped by these early messages.

Some of these deep beliefs turn into unconscious habits and biases, affecting our choices without us realizing it. For example, if someone was always told they were not good at math as a child, they may continue to struggle with numbers even as an adult, simply because of this belief.

Changing Negative Beliefs: Luckily, we can reprogram our subconscious to replace limiting beliefs with positive ones. Using affirmations, visualization, and mindfulness, we can train our minds to think in a way that supports our goals.

"The subconscious mind—processing information, shaping reality."

Our subconscious does not know the difference between reality and imagination. It accepts whatever we repeat to it. This is why many people use positive thinking and manifestation techniques to attract success and happiness into their lives.

Studies show that neuroplasticity, the brain's ability to rewire itself, allows us to change old thought patterns and replace them with new, empowering beliefs.

These internalized beliefs can either empower or limit us, influencing everything from our confidence levels to our decision-making.

Deep-seated Beliefs and Behavioral Influence:

Many of our deepest beliefs and emotions come from the subconscious mind and quietly shape how we think, feel, and act every day. For example, if a child is often told they are smart and capable, their subconscious stores this belief. As they grow, they face challenges with confidence and believe in their abilities.

On the other hand, if a child is made to feel unworthy or not good enough, their subconscious keeps this feeling. Even when they have the skills to succeed, they may doubt themselves or hesitate to take action.

These deep beliefs affect how we think, how we treat others, the choices we make, and how we handle new opportunities. Many times, people don't even realize that their subconscious is guiding their behavior.

The good news is that we can change these negative thought patterns. By becoming more aware of our beliefs, we can replace self-doubt with confidence and turn limiting thoughts into empowering ones. Psychologists say that repeating positive affirmations and practicing mindfulness can help retrain the subconscious mind, making it easier to build new habits and self-beliefs.

In Buddhist teachings, the concept of "Karma" is closely related to subconscious conditioning. Just as past actions shape future experiences, past beliefs shape present thoughts and behaviors. By changing our mindset, we can rewrite our karma and create a more positive future.

Understanding Our Inner Beliefs

Dreams and Symbols: A Glimpse into the Subconscious

Dreams act like a mirror to our subconscious mind, showing us hidden thoughts, emotions, and unresolved experiences. While our conscious mind rests during sleep, the subconscious stays active, processing information and expressing it through symbols and imagery in dreams.

These dream symbols often carry deep meanings, revealing our fears, desires, and emotions that we may not fully recognize when awake. By paying attention to recurring dreams and symbols, we can better understand our inner struggles and use them to promote personal growth and healing.

Real-Life Example: Famous artist Salvador Dalí used dreams as inspiration for his surreal paintings. He believed dreams unlocked a hidden world of creativity beyond conscious thought, leading to some of his most famous works like The Persistence of Memory.

How We See the World: The Subconscious Lens

Our subconscious mind acts as a filter, shaping how we see, feel, and react to the world. It interprets new experiences based on memories, beliefs, and emotions, which influence the way we understand reality.

Because of this, our subconscious can sometimes reinforce biases, causing us to see things not as they are, but as we expect them to be. This is why two people can experience the same event differently—their unique past experiences shape their perceptions.

Practical Example: Imagine two people watching a thunderstorm. One, who grew up loving rainy days, feels peaceful and happy, while the other, who once experienced a storm-related accident, feels anxious and fearful. Their subconscious minds interpret the same event differently based on their past experiences.

"Dreams reveal, perception shapes—our subconscious guides us."

How Our Minds Shape Reality

Our minds are like architects, building the world we live in. The conscious mind makes decisions, but the subconscious mind lays the foundation, shaping our experiences based on memories, emotions, and beliefs.

Self-Perception: The Mirror We Look Through

The subconscious mind stores everything we've ever experienced, shaping the way we see ourselves and our potential. If we constantly hear, "You are capable," we start believing it and act with confidence. But if we hear, "You're not good enough," that belief can stay with us, making us doubt our abilities—even when we're more than capable.

Historical Example: Abraham Lincoln failed in business, lost multiple elections, and faced personal struggles. Yet, his belief in his purpose helped him become one of the greatest U.S. Presidents. Had he let self-doubt win, history might have been very different.

The Invisible Script:

Our inner beliefs act like a hidden script, guiding our behavior. If someone believes they are lucky, they might notice more good opportunities. If someone believes they are unlucky, they may ignore opportunities, blaming bad luck for everything.

Real-Life Experiment: Psychologist Richard Wiseman conducted a study where people who considered themselves "lucky" were better at spotting opportunities. In a newspaper test, they noticed a hidden message offering money, while "unlucky" people, too focused on finding something specific, missed it completely. This proves that what we believe changes what we see.

The Silent Force

Most of our choices come from habits, emotions, and subconscious programming. Sometimes, we don't even realize why we make a decision—we just feel it's right or wrong.

In the Mahabharata, Karna was raised as a charioteer's son, even though he was born a prince. His subconscious belief in his low status affected his choices, making him seek validation from the wrong people. His hidden belief shaped his destiny, proving that what we believe about ourselves can be greater than reality itself.

Breaking Free from Limiting Beliefs

The moment we become aware of these hidden patterns, we take back control of our lives. Imagine replacing self-doubt with unstoppable confidence—what could you achieve?

Your subconscious mind does not judge what is true or false—it simply accepts what you tell it repeatedly. Start telling it something new.

As Henry Ford once said, "Whether you think you can, or you think you can't—you're right."

How the Subconscious Affects Our Emotions and Relationships

Making Better Choices: The Power of Awareness

Our hidden thoughts silently shape our actions. When we understand this, we can start making better, more mindful decisions instead of just acting on old patterns.

Real-Life Example: A person who grew up hearing "Money is hard to earn" might avoid taking financial risks, even when a great opportunity is right in front of them. By questioning this belief, they can make wiser financial choices instead of letting old fears control them.

Emotional Well-Being: Healing the Unseen Wounds

Our subconscious mind stores every emotion, heartbreak, and fear from our past. If left unhealed, these hidden feelings can affect our mental health, relationships, and daily happiness.

Historical Insight: After facing deep personal struggles, Winston Churchill overcame depression by engaging in painting and writing. He once said, "If you're going through hell, keep going." By confronting inner struggles rather than avoiding them, we find strength and clarity.

Breaking Free from Negative Patterns

The subconscious mind works like an autopilot, repeating past behaviors unless we consciously change them. When we reshape our beliefs, we stop repeating old mistakes and start building a life we truly want.

Practical Guide:

- Journaling – Helps bring hidden emotions to the surface.
- Affirmations – Repeating positive statements can reprogram deep beliefs.
- Self-Reflection – Question your automatic reactions. Are they based on truth or past conditioning?

Overcoming Biases: Expanding the Mind

Our hidden beliefs shape how we see others. Many prejudices and biases are just old, inherited thoughts passed down through generations. When we start questioning them, we open our minds to new perspectives and better relationships.

Historical Example: Mahatma Gandhi initially believed in class divisions, but over time, he challenged his own beliefs and became a leader of equality, proving that changing one's mindset can change the world.

Healing and Growth: Freeing Yourself from the Past

When we face our past traumas, we stop them from controlling our present and future. The subconscious holds onto old pain, but awareness, therapy, and self-reflection can help us let go and grow.

Cosmic Connection: In many spiritual teachings, the universe is said to reflect our inner world. When we heal internally, we attract better experiences externally.

Your mind is powerful—when you understand and shape your hidden thoughts, you unlock true freedom, happiness, and success.

Healing is not about forgetting the past but learning to rise above it.

The more we forgive ourselves and others, the lighter we become.

Each time we let go of a limiting belief, we create space for something better.

Growth happens when we choose love over fear and truth over illusion.

Even small shifts in thinking can lead to big changes in life.

The mind, once stretched by new awareness, never returns to its old shape.

You have the power to rewire your beliefs and rewrite your story. This journey inward leads to the greatest transformation of all—becoming who you were always meant to be.

"Transforming the subconscious—better choices, healing, and success."

Our minds play a big role in how we heal, perform, and succeed. Sometimes, just believing in something is enough to make it work—even when it has no real effect.

Placebo Effect: Healing Through Belief

A placebo is a fake treatment—like a sugar pill—that has no real medicine in it. Yet, many people feel better simply because they believe it will work.

Real-Life Example: In medical studies, some patients are given fake pills, but they still show real improvement because their mind expects healing. This is the placebo effect, proving that belief alone can influence the body.

Visualization & Affirmations: Training the Mind for Success

Our subconscious mind doesn't know the difference between real experiences and imagined ones. This is why visualizing success and repeating positive affirmations can improve performance.

Athlete Example: Many top athletes, like Michael Phelps, use mental imagery to rehearse their moves before competing. By picturing themselves winning, their subconscious prepares their bodies for real success.

How to Use This in Daily Life

Visualization: Close your eyes and picture yourself achieving your goal—whether it's a job interview, a test, or a competition.

Affirmations: Repeat positive statements like "I am confident and capable" to train your mind to believe it.

Mindset Shift: Instead of saying "I can't", start saying "I'm learning"—your subconscious will adjust accordingly.

The Takeaway

Your beliefs shape your reality. Whether it's healing through belief or achieving success through visualization, your mind is a powerful tool. Train it wisely, and you can unlock endless possibilities.

The universe responds to the energy you put out—think with doubt, and you create limits; think with faith, and you open doors.

Every great achievement begins in the mind before it

becomes reality.

Practical Uses and Healing Methods

Our minds have incredible power, and when we learn how to use them effectively, we can improve our health, habits, and overall well-being.

Hypnotherapy & Reprogramming the Subconscious

Hypnotherapy is a technique that helps people relax deeply so they can access their subconscious mind and change negative beliefs or habits. This method has been used to treat fears, anxiety, stress, and even physical pain.

Real-Life Example: Many people have overcome phobias (like fear of flying or public speaking) through hypnotherapy. By rewiring their subconscious beliefs, they change how they react to these fears in real life.

Mindfulness and Awareness: Ancient Wisdom in Modern Life

Mindfulness comes from ancient traditions like Buddhism and helps people stay present and aware. Modern science has proven that practicing mindfulness can change brain patterns, lower stress, and improve mental clarity.

Practical Use: Many companies, including Google and Apple, encourage employees to practice mindfulness to increase focus and reduce burnout. Simple habits like deep breathing and meditation can help anyone stay calm and improve decision-making.

The Power of the Mind: A Key to Transformation

The conscious and subconscious minds work together to shape who we are and what we experience.

The conscious mind helps us think, make decisions, and analyze situations. The subconscious mind runs in the background, storing memories, shaping habits, and influencing emotions.

By training our subconscious with positive thoughts and beliefs, we can change our habits and attract better outcomes in life.

Historical Insight: Famous inventor Thomas Edison used visualization and subconscious reprogramming. He would take brief naps while holding metal balls in his hands. When he fell asleep, they would drop, waking him up just as his subconscious was most active, allowing him to capture new ideas from deep within his mind.

Creating a Balanced Mind

When our conscious and subconscious minds work in harmony, we gain more control over our emotions, choices, and the future we create.

By practicing awareness, positive thinking, and subconscious reprogramming, we can shape our lives in ways we never imagined possible.

My Story

My life has been shaped by dreams and determination. I have achieved things people once thought were impossible—all because of the power of the subconscious mind.

In 2019, I was stuck in the exhausting cycle of corporate life, working over 10 hours a day, plus spending 1–2 hours commuting. It felt endless, draining my energy and motivation.

One day, I reached my breaking point. Frustrated with my exhausting job, I made a bold choice—I decided to quit and find work closer to home.

As my family needed financial support, I stayed in Gurugram, pushing through long, tiring workdays. But deep inside, I still had hope. I wanted to take back control of my time and improve my life. I knew what I wanted, but I didn't know how to get there.

Months passed, and one day, I found out that my team lead, Sumit, was working from home. That gave me an idea—a new possibility I hadn't considered before.

I found out that Sumit was not the only one with this special benefit—other team leads and managers also had it. That's when I had a realization: If I became a team lead, I could also work from home, saving time and effort.

I was determined to move up, so I focused on an internal job posting after completing 18 months at my company.

But then, reality hit me. Senior colleagues warned me that becoming a team lead could take up to 30 months. That news was discouraging, and doubt started creeping in.

Still, I refused to give up.

I wondered if I could handle 14 more months of a stressful job, giving up my personal life for a salary that didn't feel worth the effort.

Even though others doubted me, a strong voice inside refused to give up on my dreams. It kept pushing me to look for new opportunities, reminding me that I deserved a better future.

As I kept moving forward with determination, I thought about ancient wisdom, which teaches that our thoughts shape our future.

I began to understand the power of the subconscious mind even more. It guided me toward a life that matched my true dreams and desires.

One day, while watching YouTube videos I came across Joseph Murphy's book, "The Power of Your Subconscious

Mind" summary. Something about it felt important, so I quickly ordered it online to know all about the information given in the book instead of just a summary. Within a week, it arrived, and I eagerly dove into its pages, ready to learn.

Each chapter felt like a revelation, showing me that my thoughts had the power to shape my reality.

"From curiosity to discovery—the power of knowledge unfolds."

Murphy's words sparked something inside me—I realized that by training my subconscious mind, I could create the life I truly wanted.

I started practicing affirmations, visualizing my goals, and trusting the process of manifestation.

"The mind is everything. What you think, you become." –Buddha

At first, the changes were small, but as I kept going, my mindset shifted, and new opportunities started appearing. I saw for myself how changing my beliefs could bring abundance, happiness, and success into my life.

This book was more than just information—it was a guide to transformation, leading me toward a life I once only dreamed of.

The Law of Attraction was no longer just an idea—it became my truth, my guiding force, and the key to unlocking my full potential.

With each day, I saw proof that my thoughts were shaping my reality, and I learned to fully trust the process.

What once seemed impossible was now within reach, showing me that the power to create my dream life had always been inside me.

Applying the Techniques

With the knowledge from the book, I started using the techniques in my daily life.

I focused my thoughts and intentions, aligning them with the power of my subconscious mind.

"It is the mind that makes good or ill, that makes wretch or happy, rich or poor." – Edmund Spenser

Just as I started applying these techniques, the COVID-19 pandemic changed everything. Suddenly, the entire world shifted, and remote work became the new normal.

A Hidden Blessing in Tough Times

Even though the pandemic brought struggles, it also gave me an unexpected opportunity—the dream of working from home became a reality, not just for me, but for millions of people worldwide.

Though the pandemic was a global crisis, it somehow became the path through which my wish came true. The universe worked in its mysterious way, delivering my dream in a form I never expected.

Three years later, remote work is still an option. Workplaces have changed, offering more flexibility than ever before.

An Unplanned Journey

The impact of the pandemic, though unexpected, reshaped my life in ways that aligned with my subconscious desires—a journey I unknowingly set in motion.

"Life is what happens when you're busy making other plans." – Allen Saunders

This is just the beginning of the story. If you're curious about how to apply these principles in your own life, keep reading. Before going deeper, it's important to learn about brain waves and how they shape our reality. This knowledge will lay the foundation for transformation.

Coming Up Next

In the next chapters, I will share the exact steps I took—so you too can unlock the power of your subconscious mind.

CHAPTER THREE

HARMONY OF THE MIND

Introduction

The human brain is a powerful organ that processes information, controls body functions, and shapes our thoughts and emotions. One fascinating part of brain activity is the presence of electrical signals called brain waves.

Our brain helps us understand the world, react to different situations, and store memories. It influences our emotions, shaping how we respond to experiences based on past learning.

The brain also plays a key role in problem-solving and creativity, allowing us to think critically and find new solutions. Our habits are built through repeated actions, but with conscious effort, we can change negative patterns and build positive ones.

The subconscious mind works in the background, affecting our choices even when we are not aware of it. By using positive thinking and visualization, we can train our minds for success and personal growth.

When we understand how the mind works, we can take control of our thoughts and shape a life that matches our true goals and dreams.

These waves are indicative of the synchronized electrical activity of large groups of neurons working together. In this exploration, we will delve into the different types of brain waves, their mechanisms, and their potential influence on our perception of reality.

Types of Brain Waves

There are different types of brain waves, and each one is connected to how we think, feel, and act. These waves move at different speeds, measured in **Hertz (Hz).**

Some waves move fast and keep us alert and focused, while others move slowly and help us relax and think deeply. Knowing about these waves can help us focus better, reduce stress, and improve our overall mental health.

Here are the main types of brain waves:

Delta Waves (0.5-4 Hz): These are the slowest waves. They happen when we are in deep sleep and unaware of our surroundings. Delta waves help our body heal, grow, and rest properly. They are strongest in babies and young children, helping them grow quickly in body and mind.

Theta Waves (4-8 Hz): These waves appear when we are lightly sleeping, deeply relaxed, or meditating. They are linked to creativity, imagination, and intuition. People who meditate a lot often have high theta activity. These waves connect our conscious and subconscious minds, making them important for visualization and deep learning.

Alpha Waves (8-14 Hz): These waves are strong when we are calm but still awake, like when we close our eyes and take a short break. They help us stay relaxed and improve learning and creativity. Doing mindfulness exercises and deep breathing can increase alpha waves, helping to clear the mind and reduce stress.

"Brain waves shape consciousness, from sleep to awareness."

Beta Waves (14-30 Hz): These waves help us think, focus, and stay alert. They are most active when we are solving problems, making decisions, or using logic. We use beta waves the most when we are awake. However, too many beta waves can cause stress and anxiety, so it's important to keep a balance.

Gamma Waves (30-100 Hz): These are the fastest brain waves. They help with thinking, understanding, and problem-solving. Gamma waves are strongest when we have deep insights or feel very aware of things around us. Studies show that people with high gamma activity often have better focus, more compassion, and stronger brain performance.

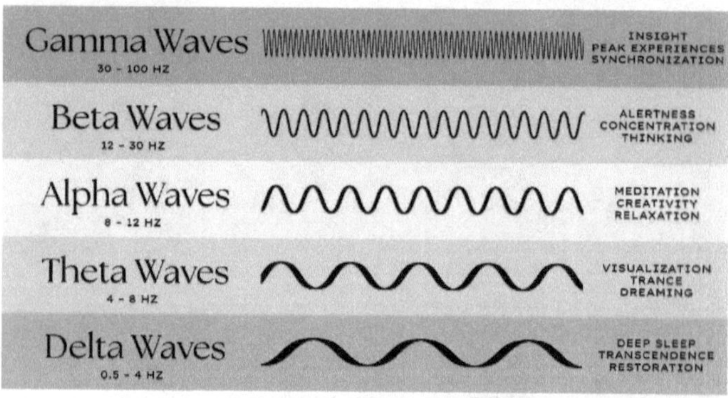

Mechanisms of Brain Waves

Our brain is constantly sending and receiving electrical signals. When millions of neurons work together in a rhythm, they create brain waves—patterns of electrical activity that shape how we think, feel, and act.

These waves can be measured using a special machine called Electroencephalography (EEG), which helps scientists understand how different brain waves affect mood, focus, creativity, and relaxation.

How to Activate and Control Brain Waves

The good news is that we can train our brains to produce specific brain waves, helping us feel more relaxed, focused, or creative. Some of the best techniques include:

1. Meditation: The Mind's Reset Button

Regular meditation has been found to increase alpha and theta waves, which promote deep relaxation, clear thinking, and creativity.

Stress Reduction: Meditation lowers stress hormones, helping us stay calm and balanced.

Emotional Stability: It improves self-awareness, allowing us to control negative emotions.

Sharper Thinking: Deep meditation can also boost gamma waves, leading to higher awareness, improved learning, and stronger memory.

2. Guided Visualization: Training the Mind Like an Athlete

When athletes visualize winning a race, their brains fire the same neural pathways as when they physically train.

This technique works for everyone—by imagining success, confidence, or relaxation, we rewire our brains to make those experiences real.

Mindfulness techniques strengthen brain connections, making it easier to replace negative thoughts with positive ones.

Over time, this rewiring helps build confidence, resilience, and a more optimistic mindset.

Consistent mental practice can lead to real improvements in performance, focus, and emotional control.

3. The Power of Consistency

Like any skill, training the brain takes practice.

Just like lifting weights builds muscles, using these techniques regularly strengthens brainwave control.

Listening to calming music or binaural beats can also help shift brain waves toward relaxation or focus.

Deep breathing and yoga enhance the effect, creating a stronger connection between the mind and body.

Journaling and gratitude exercises activate positive brain waves, helping rewire thoughts for happiness.

Final Thought: Shaping Your Reality

Over time, these techniques don't just change brain activity—they reshape how we experience life.

By aligning our thoughts and emotions with what we truly want, we create a powerful mental environment where success, happiness, and inner peace naturally grow.

Your brain is your greatest tool—train it well, and it will transform your life in ways you never imagined!

Every thought you repeat becomes a signal your brain strengthens, shaping your beliefs and actions.

With daily practice, positive thinking becomes your default setting, not just a temporary mindset.

The more you align your inner world, the more your outer world begins to reflect it.

"Neural rhythms shape the mind, meditation tunes the waves."

Binaural Beats: When you listen to two slightly different sounds in each ear, your brain creates a third sound. This sound matches a certain brain wave and can affect your mental state.

Breathwork: Breathing in a slow, deep, and steady way can change your brain waves and help you feel more relaxed or focused.

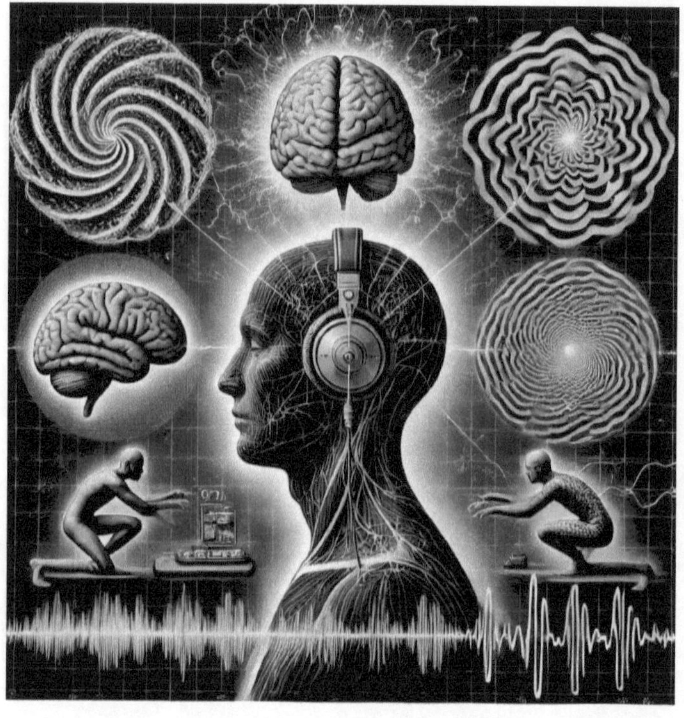

"Brain waves in harmony—sound, breath, and technology unite."

Biofeedback: This method tracks body functions like heart rate or muscle tension and shows you the results. It helps you learn how to control these functions on your own.

Neurofeedback: Like biofeedback, this method shows your brain activity in real time. It helps you train your brain to stay in a healthy and balanced state.

Brain waves have a big effect on our lives. Keeping them balanced is important for a healthy mind, clear thinking, and emotional well-being. Here's how different brain waves help us:

Better Focus and Attention: Beta waves help us stay alert and concentrate, which is important for tasks that need full attention.

More Creativity: Theta waves, which appear during deep relaxation and creative thinking, help boost imagination and problem-solving skills.

Improved Sleep: Delta waves are important for deep sleep, which helps the body and mind rest and recover.

Less Stress: Alpha waves bring a calm and peaceful feeling, helping to reduce stress and improve overall well-being.

Scientists have made an amazing discovery: When brain waves match the universe's energy, new possibilities open up. When our minds connect with cosmic energy, our reality can change.

The key mechanisms underlying brain waves include

Neurons Working Together: Brain waves happen when many brain cells (neurons) work at the same time. When they send signals together, they create electric waves that can be measured on the head.

The Thalamus Controls Brain Waves: The thalamus, an important part of the brain, helps control how fast or strong brain waves are. It acts like a gatekeeper, deciding what information goes to different parts of the brain.

Brain Chemicals (Neurotransmitters): Certain brain chemicals, like dopamine, serotonin, and GABA, affect brain waves. If these chemicals are not balanced, they can change how we feel and think, sometimes leading to mental health problems.

Brain Waves Can Be Changed by Outside Things: Light, sound, and meditation can change brain waves. This is called "brain wave entrainment." For example, listening to special sounds like binaural beats can help the brain match a certain wave pattern, which may improve focus or relaxation.

How Brain Waves Affect Our Reality

The relationship between brain waves and our perception of reality is a multifaceted and intricate subject.

Neuroscientists, psychologists, and even ancient philosophical and spiritual traditions have explored the potential impact of brain waves on consciousness and the human experience.

Altered States of Consciousness:

a) Meditation: Research has shown that meditation practices, which often involve manipulation of brain waves, can lead to altered states of consciousness.

Increased theta and alpha activity during meditation is associated with a heightened sense of awareness, relaxation, and inner tranquility.

Deep meditation can induce profound spiritual experiences, enhancing intuition and expanding perception beyond ordinary awareness.

Certain breathing techniques and mindfulness exercises can shift brain wave patterns, facilitating deep relaxation and emotional healing.

Regular meditation can improve memory, attention, and emotional balance by enhancing brain plasticity.

Over time, these changes support greater self-awareness and a lasting sense of inner peace.

"Meditation and brain waves—unlocking altered states of consciousness."

Prolonged meditative states may also enhance neuroplasticity, allowing the brain to rewire itself for greater clarity and resilience.

Practices such as sound healing and binaural beats can further influence brain wave activity, guiding the mind into deeper states of consciousness.

Research on substances like psilocybin and LSD shows that they can change how the brain works, creating different states of awareness. These drugs increase connections between different parts of the brain and change gamma wave activity, which affects perception and thinking.

Better Learning and Thinking:

Flow State: This is a mental state where a person is fully focused and performing at their best.

"Flow state and deep sleep—unlocking focus and memory retention."

It happens when the brain shifts to more theta and alpha waves, creating a balance between deep relaxation and sharp attention. This state helps with creativity, learning, and problem-solving.

Stronger Memory:

When we are in deep sleep, our brain produces delta waves. During this time, the brain works to organize and store memories. Everything we learn during the day is processed and saved so we can remember it for a long time.

Emotional Balance and Well-being

Brain Training with Neurofeedback:
Neurofeedback is a method that helps people control their brain waves. It is used to treat anxiety, depression, and focus problems by encouraging healthy brain activity.

How It Works:

People get real-time updates on their brain activity, helping them shift into a calmer and more focused state.

This therapy improves thinking skills, emotional stability, and overall mental strength.

Combining neurofeedback with relaxation exercises can further reduce stress and help control emotions better.

Keeping Brain Waves Balanced:

Too many beta waves can lead to stress and anxiety.

A good balance of alpha and theta waves promotes peace, creativity, and emotional clarity.

Mindfulness practices like deep breathing and visualization can help keep emotions stable.

The Role of Sleep and Environment:

Deep sleep (delta waves) helps process emotions and recover from stress.

Spending time in nature, listening to calming music, or using positive affirmations can also improve brain wave balance and bring a sense of peace.

By learning to manage brain waves, people can gain better control over their emotions and live a more balanced and happy life.

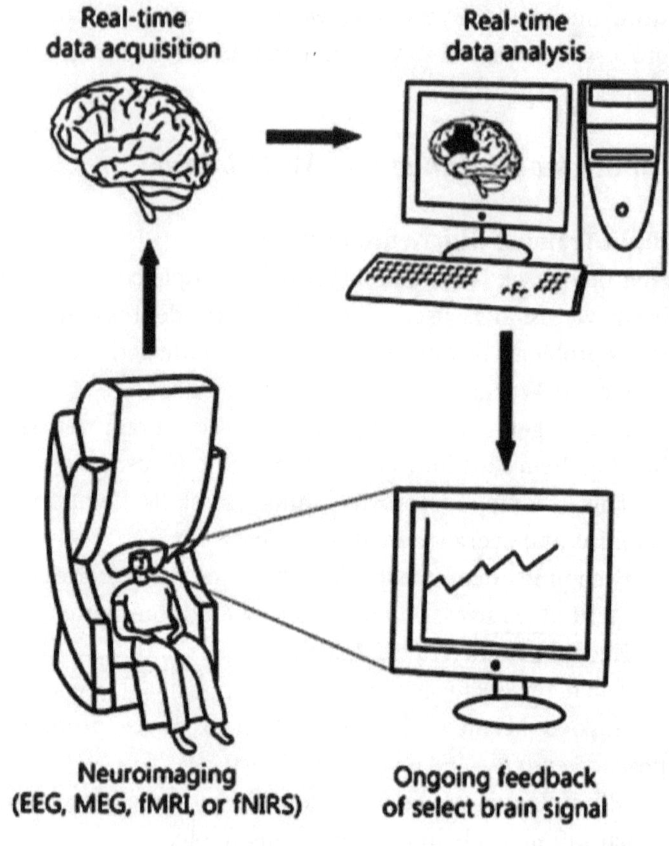

"Neurofeedback—Harnessing Brain Signals for Enhanced Mental Performance." ???

Emotional Strength (Resilience):
Studies show that alpha brain waves help people stay emotionally strong. Those who naturally produce more

alpha waves can handle stress better and control their emotions more easily. This means they are less likely to feel overwhelmed and can stay calm even in tough situations.

4. Spiritual and Transcendent Experiences

For thousands of years, ancient texts and spiritual teachings have spoken about deep states of awareness and higher consciousness. People have used meditation, prayer, and deep thinking to change their brain wave patterns, helping them feel more connected to something greater than themselves.

How Spiritual Practices Affect Brain Waves

Chanting, breathwork, and deep meditation can increase gamma waves, leading to powerful insights and a clearer mind.

Many spiritual leaders and mystics have described moments of deep unity and enlightenment, which are linked to shifts in brain waves.

In these states, people often feel time slows down, inner peace grows, and they feel deeply connected to the universe. Some even describe a sensation of dissolving boundaries, as if they are merging with the vastness of existence. These heightened states of awareness often bring a profound sense of wisdom and inner transformation.

Near-Death Experiences (NDEs):

Some people who have come close to death report life-changing spiritual experiences. Scientists believe these events change brain wave activity, leading to a strong feeling of connection and deep awareness.

During an NDE, people often describe:

- Vivid visions and meeting spiritual beings

- A feeling of overwhelming love and peace
- A sense of leaving their body and seeing the world from above

Lucid Dreaming and Out-of-Body Experiences:
Theta and delta waves are believed to play a big role in lucid dreaming (when you know you are dreaming and can control it).

Some people also report out-of-body experiences, where they feel like they are floating outside their body.
Real-Life Examples of Famous People:
Nikola Tesla – The Power of Visualization
The famous inventor Nikola Tesla often spoke about seeing entire inventions in his mind before building them.
His ability to deeply visualize ideas may be linked to high theta wave activity, which helps with imagination and deep thinking.
He believed the mind was a powerful tool that could shape reality.
Tesla once said, "If you want to find the secrets of the universe, think in terms of energy, frequency, and vibration."

Albert Einstein – The Power of Deep Thought
Einstein was known for entering a dream-like state when solving problems, often using daydreaming and visualization.
Scientists believe he had high levels of alpha and theta waves, helping him reach deep insights.
He trusted his inner world more than logic at times.
Einstein himself admitted, "Imagination is more important than knowledge."

Conclusion

Exploring different brain wave states can lead to personal growth, self-discovery, and a deeper understanding of life. Through meditation, mindfulness, and spiritual practices, people can experience greater peace, creativity, and higher awareness, just like many great minds and spiritual leaders throughout history.

"Bridging science and spirituality—brain waves and transcendence."

From deep thinking and creativity to better focus and emotional balance, studying brain waves helps us understand how the mind works and how it connects to the world.

As we explore science, psychology, and spirituality, we see that ancient wisdom and modern research work together to give us a complete picture of human consciousness.

Richard's Odyssey

In the quiet town of Harmony Springs, a man named Richard Turner faced a battle that most would call impossible. He was diagnosed with a rare and aggressive cancer—one that defied every treatment doctors threw at it.

When hospitals and medicine failed him, Richard did something most wouldn't dare—he chose to fight in a way few understood.

One evening, as he sat alone, staring at the endless sky, a thought struck him like a bolt of lightning. He recalled an ancient truth he had once read:
"As a man thinketh in his heart, so is he."

Could his mind be the key? Could he somehow reprogram his body to heal? The idea consumed him, not as a desperate man grasping at straws, but as a seeker unlocking a door to the unknown.

The Dance with the Universe

He immersed himself in the world of energy, vibration, and frequencies. If the universe had a rhythm, a frequency of healing, he would find a way to match it. Binaural beats, meditation, deep breathing, visualization—these became his weapons.

Each morning, he closed his eyes and whispered, **"Be still and know that I am."**

He imagined his cells vibrating with cosmic energy, tuning in like an orchestra adjusting to a perfect note. He wasn't just visualizing health; he was living it in his mind before his body could catch up.

The Power of the Mind

In his silent sanctuary, Richard harnessed gamma waves, those linked to superior thinking, deep intuition, and—perhaps—healing. He breathed deeply, entering the elusive theta state, where the body's most powerful healing processes take place.

With every breath, every moment of stillness, he whispered another affirmation, as if commanding his very cells to obey.

"Renew your mind."

And the most astonishing thing? Something began to change.

The Miracle Unfolds

Days turned to weeks, and weeks into months. What started as a whisper of hope became a roaring force inside him. His doctors were baffled—his scans showed signs of improvement. Tumors that were once growing started to shrink.

Richard didn't claim magic, nor did he reject science. He simply stepped into a space where both could meet—where mind, body, and universe became one.

His story wasn't just about survival; it was about unlocking the hidden power within us all.

For Richard, healing wasn't just about fighting cancer. It was about rewriting the rules of what we believe is possible.

The constant pain that once ruled his life started to fade, replaced by newfound energy and strength. As word of Richard's recovery spread, people everywhere became curious. Some were skeptics, while others were seeking alternative paths to healing.

Science Meets Spirituality

Scientists and researchers, fascinated by this hidden link between the brain and healing, started exploring how thoughts, energy, and brain waves could affect the body.

The ancient wisdom, "As you sow, so shall you reap," suddenly made perfect sense. Their studies uncovered a shocking truth—the power of the mind was far greater than anyone had imagined.

They found that people who learned to control their brain waves through meditation, visualization, and deep focus experienced incredible changes. Their health improved, their minds became sharper, and their overall well-being soared.

Even more astonishing, some patients, just like Richard, defied the odds. They didn't just feel better; some even saw remission from serious illnesses—proving that the mind and body are deeply connected in ways science is only beginning to understand.

A New Era of Healing

This discovery changed everything. It bridged the gap between science and spirituality, showing that the mind and body are connected in ways we never fully understood before and if we align both in one direction, we can conquer the unimaginable.

Richard's Story Became a Beacon of Hope

His journey was no longer just about his battle with illness—it became a powerful message for anyone facing life's toughest struggles.

A Living Proof of Possibility

Richard was no longer just a patient. He was living proof that the human mind holds extraordinary power over the body. His story inspired thousands to:

Unlock their inner strength

Question the limits of medicine

Seek new ways to heal and thrive

His experience showed the world that we are not just victims of fate. We have the power to rewrite our reality, reshape our thoughts, and create a future filled with health, hope, and transformation.

As his journey unfolded, it seemed to echo an ancient truth:

"Know ye not that ye are the temple of God?"

This was more than just a spiritual idea—it was a powerful reminder that inside each of us lies unimaginable strength, waiting to be awakened.

Your Life, Your Power

Now, imagine for a moment that you, like Richard, have the power to rewrite your story. What if healing, success, and happiness were all within reach, waiting for you to tune into the right frequency?

What if your thoughts could shape your reality?

What if you could reprogram your subconscious to heal, grow, and thrive?

What if you could tap into the universe's energy and create the life you desire?

You don't need a miracle—you need a shift in mindset.

Imagine your life as a musical masterpiece—you hold the conductor's baton. The way you think, feel and believe shapes the melody of your existence.

When you align yourself with positive energy, gratitude, and belief, you don't just live—you thrive.

Richard's journey wasn't just about healing; it was about discovering the limitless potential within.

Now, it's your turn.

Will you let life control your story, or will you take the pen and write a masterpiece of transformation, growth, and infinite possibilities?

"Your life, your script—sync with the cosmic rhythm."

CHAPTER FOUR

THE HERMETIC CODE

Introduction

Hermeticism is a deep and secret way of thinking and believing that comes from ancient Egypt. People often connect it to a mystical figure called Hermes Trismegistus.

This spiritual system includes many kinds of knowledge, like alchemy (changing metals), astrology (studying stars), magic, and deep wisdom. Its teachings have strongly influenced many religions, philosophies, and hidden traditions throughout history.

In this journey, we will look into where Hermeticism came from, its main ideas, different parts of it, and why it still inspires people today.

Origins of Hermeticism

The beginning of Hermeticism is lost in ancient history, making it hard to know exactly when it started. However, experts believe it began in Hellenistic Egypt during the 2nd and 3rd centuries CE.

The legendary Hermes Trismegistus is seen as the main figure of Hermeticism. He is often described as a mix of the Greek god Hermes and the Egyptian god Thoth.

"Unveiling the origins of Hermeticism—wisdom of the ancients."

Hermes Trismegistus is believed to be the writer of the Corpus Hermeticum, a group of philosophical and mystical writings that became the foundation of Hermetic teachings.

These texts, written in Greek and linked to Hermes, include many different types of knowledge, such as the nature of reality (metaphysics), the universe (cosmology), magic, and deep spiritual wisdom.

Core Principles of Hermeticism

1. The Principle of Correspondence: "As above, so below." This means that everything in the big universe (macrocosm) is connected to everything in the small world (microcosm), including individuals. Understanding one helps us understand the other.

2. The Principle of Mentalism states that everything comes from the mind. The idea is that thoughts and consciousness shape reality. A universal mind creates the universe, and our thinking influences the world around us.

3. The Principle of Vibration: Everything is always moving. Nothing stays still—everything vibrates at a certain speed. By understanding vibrations, one can gain control over different forces, even in alchemy (changing materials and energy).

4. The Principle of Polarity: Opposites are connected. Things that seem opposite—like light and dark, hot and cold—are different versions of the same thing. Learning to balance opposites helps us understand life's deeper truths.

5. The Principle of Rhythm: Life moves in cycles. Just like seasons change, tides rise and fall, and moods shift, everything follows a pattern. Learning these rhythms helps people flow with life instead of fighting against it.

6. The Principle of Cause and Effect: Every action reacts. Nothing happens by chance. Everything we do, think, or say has a result. This principle teaches responsibility for

our choices and how they shape our future.

7. The Principle of Gender: Masculine and feminine energy exists in everything. These energies are not just about gender but balance in all things—action and stillness, logic and intuition. Understanding both leads to personal and spiritual growth. When these energies are in harmony, we feel more whole, peaceful, and aligned with our true self.

"Unlocking the wisdom of the Seven Hermetic Principles."

The Different Branches of Hermeticism

Over time, Hermeticism has changed and grown into different forms, each focusing on different parts of its teachings. Some of the most important branches include:

Philosophical Hermeticism:

This branch studies the deep ideas behind Hermeticism, such as the nature of reality, the universe, and consciousness. It tries to answer big questions about existence, the soul, and the connection between all things. Many followers believe that true knowledge comes from both study and direct experience, blending intellect with spiritual intuition. This philosophy encourages seekers to explore the hidden forces behind life and to develop a deeper sense of inner harmony.

Alchemy:

Alchemy is not just about turning metals into gold—it is also about changing and improving the mind and soul. It represents a personal journey of growth, purification, and self-discovery. Alchemists believe that by improving their thoughts and emotions, they can reach a higher state of awareness, just like turning lead into gold is a symbol of self-mastery. Many alchemical texts describe the "Great Work" as a lifelong process of refining one's character and unlocking inner potential.

Astrology:

Hermetic astrology is based on the idea that the universe (macrocosm) and people (microcosm) are connected. It teaches that planetary movements affect human life and events on Earth. By understanding the positions of planets and their energy, people can align themselves with the universe's rhythms, helping with spiritual growth and life choices. This follows the ancient

Hermetic saying, "As above, so below," meaning that what happens in the stars is reflected in life on Earth. Others use it as a tool for self-reflection, guiding them toward greater awareness and alignment with universal forces.

- **Magical Hermeticism:** This branch focuses on ceremonial magic, rituals, and calling upon spiritual beings for personal and spiritual growth. Practitioners use symbols, chants, and sacred practices to connect with higher forces and influence reality. It is based on the belief that human consciousness and divine energy can work together to bring change and transformation.
- **Christian Hermeticism:** This branch combines Hermetic ideas with Christian beliefs, showing how they share deep spiritual truths.

It finds similarities between Hermetic teachings and the Christian faith, such as the ideas of inner transformation, divine wisdom, and the connection between God and the human soul. Many followers believe that Christianity and Hermeticism both seek spiritual enlightenment and a deeper understanding of the divine.

Naming of Hermeticism

The word "Hermeticism" comes from Hermes Trismegistus, the legendary figure connected to this tradition.

The name has its roots in the Greek god Hermes, who was known as a messenger between gods and humans.

The title "Trismegistus" means "thrice-great," showing that Hermes was seen as great in three ways:

As a king (a ruler),

As a priest (a spiritual guide),

As a philosopher (a seeker of wisdom).

The word "Hermeticism" became popular during the Renaissance, a time when people became interested again in old mystical traditions.

During this period, scholars and thinkers found and translated Hermetic texts, bringing Hermetic ideas into many spiritual and intellectual movements.

Conclusion

Hermeticism is a rich and lasting tradition that brings together philosophy, spirituality, and mystical practices. It began in ancient Egypt, is linked to the legendary Hermes Trismegistus, and teaches the deep connection between all things in the universe. These ideas have had a strong influence on Western mystical traditions.

The many different branches of Hermeticism show how flexible and timeless it is, attracting seekers of wisdom throughout history.

As people continue to explore its teachings, Hermeticism remains a guiding light for those looking for spiritual knowledge and a deeper understanding of life.

In ancient times, Hermetic teachings were seen as a bridge between the universe and human existence. The belief that "As above, so below" showed that everything happening in the cosmos is also reflected in human life.

Ancient scholars, priests, and mystics studied celestial movements, believing that the stars and planets influenced human destiny.

Hermeticists believed that the universe was alive, and made of energy and vibrations, just like human thoughts and emotions. This led them to practice alchemy, astrology, and sacred rituals to align themselves with universal forces.

The connection between human consciousness and the cosmic mind was a key idea in Hermetic traditions, teaching that by understanding nature, one could understand themselves.

Temples and sacred sites in Egypt and Greece were built using Hermetic principles, designed to capture cosmic energy and enhance spiritual awareness. Initiates spent years learning how to master their mind, body, and spirit, believing that true wisdom came from balancing all three.

By tapping into these universal laws, ancient seekers believed they could transform their inner world, just like alchemists transformed metals. This deep understanding of human and cosmic connection made Hermeticism one of the most profound and enduring teachings of all time.

CHAPTER FIVE

Empowering Echoes

Introduction

So far, we have studied the interconnection of the Universe with us, how the subconscious and conscious minds work together to create a better life, and how we can sync our brain waves with the universe's energy to achieve any goal.

Now, let's look at the first technique that will help you achieve the best you deserve. Manifestation and affirmation are powerful concepts that delve into the intricate relationship between thought, language, and the shaping of our reality.

By consciously directing our thoughts and emotions, we can harness the energy around us to attract success, happiness, and abundance into our lives.

The key lies in aligning our intentions with unwavering belief, reinforcing them with positive affirmations, and taking inspired action toward our goals.

Manifestation: Unveiling the Power of Thought

Manifestation is based on the belief that thoughts have a real effect on the outside world. It says that by keeping one's thoughts and wishes on a certain desire or result, a person can make that wish come true. This idea agrees with the thought that the mind and awareness help shape the things we go through.

At its heart, manifestation means using one's energy and attention toward a clear goal.

People who believe in this idea say that the universe answers our thoughts, feelings, and wishes, making outside events match what we feel inside.

This means there is a deep connection between a person and the big forces of the universe.

Affirmation: The Power of Positive Language

Affirmation, on the other hand, is about using good words to build strong beliefs and create a happy way of thinking. It works on the idea that the words we say shape our thoughts, and our thoughts then affect what we do and what happens to us.

Affirmations are short, positive sentences that people say to themselves to change their deep thoughts into good beliefs.

The power of affirmation comes from its ability to stop negative thoughts and help create a way of thinking that leads to success and happiness. By always saying positive words, people try to make their mind a place that helps them reach their dreams and goals.

Scientists have found that positive affirmations turn on parts of the brain that help people feel worthy and motivated, making them see life in a better way.

To work best, affirmations should be said in the present time, as if what a person wants is already real. This helps the brain believe it is happening.

When used with imagination, affirmations become even stronger, creating a clear picture in the mind that brings together thoughts, feelings, and actions to reach a goal.

"Affirmations reshape the mind—confidence, success, and growth."

"Don't hear, speak or see anything bad"
"This shall too pass"
"You are different from others"

These are some of the examples of positive affirmations that give hope, confidence, and courage to face any challenges in life.

While these practices may not be universally proven, many find them beneficial in cultivating a positive mindset and pursuing personal goals.

Here's a step-by-step guide on how to practice manifestation and affirmations and the potential effects they can have on life:

- **Find Areas to Improve:** Look at parts of your life where you want good changes. This could be about self-worth, health, relationships, or work. Knowing these areas is important to make strong affirmations.
- **Set Clear Goals:** First, decide and clearly say what you want to bring into your life. It can be personal growth, happiness, or clear goals like a better job or stronger relationships. The important thing is to be clear and sure. The goal must be very clear, or it might not work well.
- **Make Positive Sentences:** Create affirmations that push away bad thoughts. If you have trouble feeling good about yourself, say things like "I am strong and deserve success." Your affirmations should be positive, in the present, and clear.
- **Feel Thankful:** Be grateful for what you already have. A thankful mind can bring more good things into your life. Often, take time to see and enjoy the good things you

have.

- **Take Action:** Manifestation is not just about wishing; you must do things. Take steps that match your dreams. This can mean meeting new people, learning new things, or changing small daily habits.
- **Trust the Process:** Believe deeply that the universe is helping you. Doubt and negative thoughts can slow down the process. Trust that with time and effort, what you want will happen.

"Define, focus, manifest—clarity turns dreams into reality."

- **Repeat Often:** Doing it again and again is important. Say your affirmations every day, best in the morning or before sleeping. Repeating them helps put these good thoughts deep in your mind.
- **Stay Happy and Open:** Keep a happy mind and be open. Accept your affirmations with hope and believe that good changes are not just possible but will surely happen.

- **Check and Change:** Keep looking at your affirmations and goals. As life changes, what you want may also change. Make sure your affirmations match your current dreams.
- **Be Patient:***"Rome was not built in a day,"* and your dreams also won't come true in one night. It takes time, and the universe will show you the way to get what you wish for.

Manifestation and affirmations take time. You may not see quick results, but waiting is important. Believe in the right time and keep working toward your dreams.

How This Technique Affects Our Life

- **Change in Thinking:** Using manifestation and affirmation can bring a big change in how we think. By focusing on good thoughts and goals, people often feel more hopeful and see life in a better way. This is a proven way of reprogramming our subconscious mind with positive thinking and a hope to move in the right direction.
- **Better Focus and Awareness:** Practicing these methods often helps people understand their goals and what is important. This makes them make better decisions and notice changes that match what they want. By focusing on the relevant things we manage to avoid the distractions in our life.
- **Bringing Good Energy:** The idea of bringing good things by thinking good thoughts is a key part of manifestation. Many people believe that staying positive helps attract good situations and chances in life.

- **More Confidence and Self-Belief:** Affirmations help in making people feel more sure of themselves. When people say good things about themselves often, they start believing in themselves more and feel more valuable.

"Manifestation transforms—focus, confidence, and resilience in action."

- **Drive and Taking Action:** Manifestation is not just about thinking; it also means taking real steps toward your goals. These methods can push people to follow their dreams, leading to real progress and success.

- **Stronger Inner Strength:** A positive way of thinking, built through manifestation and affirmations, can help people stay strong during hard times. They may start seeing problems in a better way, helping them handle challenges with more power and patience.

Ancient Roots and Resemblances

Manifestation and affirmation have been around for a long time, appearing in many old beliefs and spiritual teachings. The idea of manifestation is like the law of attraction, which says that similar things attract each other.

Old teachings like Hermeticism talked about mentalism—the belief that the mind is the main reality and that thoughts create the world around us.

In Eastern beliefs like Hinduism and Buddhism, thoughts and intentions are very important. Practices like meditation and mindfulness show this idea. The Vedantic belief in 'Brahman' as the highest truth connects to the idea that awareness shapes life.

Affirmations have also been used in ancient ways, like positive statements in Sanskrit texts and mantras in Hinduism and Buddhism. Repeating good words to create a better way of thinking is a shared idea in many cultures and spiritual paths.

These ancient teachings suggest that our thoughts are not just passive ideas but active forces that shape our experiences. Many cultures have used chants, prayers, and sacred texts to reinforce positive thinking and bring desired outcomes.

Even today, modern psychology and self-help movements continue to support these age-old principles, showing that the power of thoughts and affirmations remains as relevant as ever.

"Ancient wisdom of manifestation—thoughts shaping reality across traditions."

Affirmations work best when they are made personal, said in the present, and use positive words.

By making them part of daily life, people can slowly change the way they think and build a happier and stronger mind.

Saying them every day helps remove negative thoughts and replace them with hope and confidence. Over time, this practice can improve self-belief and make people feel more in control of their lives. Affirmations also help people stay focused on their goals and believe in their power to achieve them.

The Science Behind Manifestation and Affirmation

While manifestation and affirmation come from old beliefs, today, they mix spiritual ideas with science.

Brain studies show that positive thinking affects how the mind works and helps mental health.

The brain has neuroplasticity, meaning it can change and grow by making new connections. This supports the idea that repeating good thoughts and affirmations can change the way we think and act.

Studies on the placebo effect show that what we believe can change our body and health.

The observer effect in quantum physics says that just watching something can change it. This is similar to the idea that our thoughts and awareness can shape reality.

This mix of science and spirituality shows that belief, focus, and positive thoughts can create real changes in life.

Challenges and Criticisms

While manifestation and affirmation are well-liked, some people do not fully believe in them.

They say that thinking alone cannot control everything in life because life is complex.

They point out that outside factors, social systems, and money situations also shape a person's life.

Some also warn about toxic positivity, where people hide their real feelings just to stay positive.

It is important to accept problems but still stay hopeful, as this helps in growing and improving life in a balanced way.

Cultural and Ethical Considerations

The huge popularity of manifestation and affirmation has led to taking these ideas from their original cultures and turning them into products to sell.

Taking these beliefs away from their true history and meaning can make them less deep and important.

It is important to respect where these ideas come from and understand their cultural value.

Some people also worry about using manifestation to push materialism or false hopes.

If people only think about personal success without caring about others, it can lead to a selfish way of thinking that may hurt society.

My Story

In Chapter 1, I shared how I got a work-from-home job, saving two hours of travel and reducing rent costs. Now, I want to tell you how manifestation and affirmations helped me reach my next goal.

In August 2021, after working 10 hours a day, I felt I needed a break from my career. So, I decided to try a new affirmation as a test. I wrote on paper:

"Thank you for giving me a work-from-home job with little or no work."

For two weeks, I kept saying this affirmation, but nothing happened, and I started feeling a bit low.

Then, a few days later, I got a call from an HR team at a new company.

They wanted to interview me, and I got excited about leaving my current job for a better-paying role at XYZ company.

During the interview, I forgot about my manifestation practice and just focused on getting the new job.

Luckily, I passed the interview and waited excitedly for my offer letter.

Meanwhile, a friend who had worked at XYZ company called and said, "You'll love it at XYZ; there's no work pressure."

This shocked me, and I started believing that my manifestation was working.

During my notice period, I decided to try one more manifestation. In my diary, I wrote:

"Thank you for giving me a permanent work-from-home job with weekends off and a $60,000 salary."

I felt doubtful about manifesting a 400% salary increase, but I kept saying my affirmations.

A few days later, my friend Aarif called just to chat. I told him about my new manifestation.

Aarif advised me to check Crossover.com, a website that pays in dollars.

I was amazed to find many job postings that matched my profile, all offering a $60,000 salary.

This was a big moment for me, proving that manifestation and affirmations work.

Even though I did not get the job, I will explain why in the final chapter.

So, stay tuned for the full story...

CHAPTER SIX

MANIFESTATION MOSAIC

Introduction

Imagination is like watching a movie with your eyes closed—a stream of pictures flowing in the mind, where seeing is the most powerful of the five senses.

With every thought, the mind conjures vivid images, making dreams, memories, and wishes feel tangible. Athletes, artists, and great thinkers have employed this technique for many years to enhance their skills and achieve their objectives.

When practiced with clear intention, imagination becomes a bridge between dreams and reality, transforming simple thoughts into real experiences.

The more vividly one imagines, the stronger the brain registers it as a real possibility, making it easier to turn vision into reality.

"Close your eyes and see the flow of pictures – friends, family, worries, and dreams. Now, try to focus on one picture. Let's find the magic as we explore the Art of

Visualization."

Why Use Visualization?

"Visualization is my favorite and most powerful technique. Focusing on it can bring the results you want. But how is it better than affirmations? If visualization is the player, then affirmations are like the cheerleaders of the game."

Creating a Mental Picture

"Think of it like making a picture in your mind – a workout for your brain. See your goal, break it into steps, and watch it become real."

Visualization is more than just feeling positive; it uses all senses. It is the belief that good thoughts create good things.

Using the Senses

"Visualization is not just happy thinking; it brings your senses into action. Imagine success – passing that job interview, getting that promotion. Whether in personal life or work, visualization can turn dreams into real life."

Feel the emotions of success—the excitement of achievement, the confidence in your voice, and the pride in your efforts.

See the details of your goal, hear the sounds around you, and even imagine the scents and textures of your success.

The more real it feels in your mind, the more powerfully your brain accepts it as possible.

As Albert Einstein said:

"Imagination is more important than knowledge. Knowledge has limits, but imagination touches the whole world, pushing us forward and creating change."

Use the power of visualization to wake up the hidden possibilities in your mind.

"Visualization activates all senses—seeing, hearing, touching, tasting, and smelling success."

Benefits

- Clarity in decision-making.
- A step-by-step guide to achieving your goals.
- Improved mental health.
- Enhanced focus power.

Now, let's take a look at the ultimate tool for visualizing. The Vision Board Technique.

As the name suggests, vision boards are all about crafting a visual representation of your dreams. **So, let's start.**

Stage1: Creating the Vision Board

Step1:Define Goals

Clearly articulate your short-term and long-term goals. These could be related to career, relationships, health, or personal development. Be specific and detailed about what you want to achieve to give your mind a clear direction.

Write your goals in the present tense, as if they are already happening, to reinforce belief and motivation.

Break big goals into smaller, achievable steps to stay focused and track progress easily.

Step2: Gather material

Gather the required materials that you will need to represent your goals.

Poster Board or Canvas – This is the foundation where you will bring your dreams to life. Choose a size that fits your space, whether large or small.

Magazines, Images, and Quotes – Gather pictures and words that represent your dreams, goals, and inspirations—such as career, home, health, or lifestyle.

Glue, Scissors, and Markers – These basic tools help you cut, arrange, and design your vision board. Markers allow you to add affirmations or goal reminders.

Colored Pens or Pencils – Use colors to highlight important goals. Different colors can represent different emotions—blue for peace, red for passion, and green for growth.

Stickers and Decorative Elements – Add stickers, washi tape, or glitter to make your board exciting and visually appealing. The more engaging it looks, the more motivated you'll be.

Affirmations and Quotes – Write empowering words like "Success," "Abundance," "Happiness" or a personal affirmation such as "I am capable of achieving my dreams."

Personal Photos – Include photos of yourself or loved ones to create an emotional connection with your vision. Seeing familiar faces reminds you why your dreams matter.

Timelines for Goals – Add dates or milestones to create a sense of urgency and motivation, like "Achieve my dream job by December 2025."

Sections for Different Goals – Divide your board into categories like career, health, relationships, finances, and personal growth to stay organized.

Make It Fun and Personal – Your vision board should be a reflection of you, so make it beautiful, inspiring, and meaningful to keep yourself engaged and focused.

Choose pictures that feel personal and inspiring, making it easier to connect emotionally with your vision.

Ensure the images reflect the exact lifestyle, success, or experiences you want to manifest.

Step3: Create Collage

Cut out images and quotes and arrange them on the board. Use glue to secure them in place and make sure they are relevant to your goals. Choosing the right images is important as they will help in mirroring the dream in your mind.

"Crafting your vision—gather, create, and manifest your dreams."

Step4: Add Personal Touch

Use markers, colored pens, or pencils to add creative elements that make your vision board uniquely yours. Write affirmations, motivational quotes, or specific details about your goals. You can also add doodles, stickers, or personal notes that inspire and uplift you. The more personal and meaningful it is, the stronger the emotional connection to your aspirations.

Step5: Place in a Visible Location

Choose a place where your vision board will be seen daily—such as your bedroom, workspace, or near your mirror. Seeing it frequently will keep your goals at the forefront of your mind, reinforcing your intentions and encouraging positive action.

Step6: Engage with Your Vision Board Daily

Spend a few minutes each day looking at your vision board. As you do, visualize yourself achieving each goal. Feel the emotions associated with success—happiness, excitement, gratitude. The more vividly you can picture it, the stronger the impact on your subconscious mind.

Step7: Update and Evolve

As your goals grow and evolve, update your vision board to reflect your new aspirations. Remove things that no longer resonate and add fresh inspirations that align with your current desires. A vision board is a living representation of your dreams—keep it dynamic and meaningful.

Step8: Believe and Take Action

A vision board is not just about visualization—it's about action. Every day, take small steps toward your goals. Let your board be a source of motivation and a reminder that success is within your reach. Combine belief with effort, and watch your manifestations come to life.

Display your vision board in a place where you can see it daily. This constant visual reminder reinforces your goals and strengthens the connection between your mind and your aspirations.

Stage2: Visualize

Now sit down, relax, and imagine your future. Close your eyes and let your mind wander into the life you dream of. Breathe deeply and visualize yourself already living that reality. Feel the joy, excitement, and satisfaction as if it's happening right now.

See-through those dreams the future you desire. Picture yourself achieving your goals effortlessly. Walk through your dream life in your mind—where are you? What do you see? Who is with you? How do you feel in this moment of success?

Example: If you dream of riding your favorite bike, imagine gripping the handlebars, feeling the wind on your face, and hearing the roar of the engine as you cruise down the open road. If you aspire to own a luxury car, visualize yourself behind the wheel, feeling the smooth drive, admiring the sleek design, and experiencing the pride of ownership. If your goal is to buy a big house, walk through its grand entrance in your mind and explore the spacious rooms.

Engage all your senses. Smell the air and immerse yourself in the experience. The more real it feels in your mind, the more powerful its manifestation becomes.

Hold onto this vision. Let it guide and inspire you every day. Your dreams are already forming in the unseen—believe in them, take action, and watch them turn into reality.

Stage 3: Repetitions

Now, every day for at least 30 minutes sit down in front of your vision board, close your eyes, put on some calming meditative music, and visualize those dreams coming true.

To make it more effective you can go and have a test drive of the car/ bike and this will give you a glimpse of how your life will be once the dream is fulfilled.

Important Tip: In the beginning, keep it simple and start slow. Having too many dreams on your board might dilute your focus. Start with one wish at a time; once it's a habit, add more.

Origin of Visualization Manifestation Technique

The roots of the Visualization Manifestation Technique can be traced back to various ancient cultures and philosophical traditions that recognized the profound connection between thoughts and reality.

The Law of Attraction, a fundamental principle in this technique, originates from the Hermetic teachings, particularly the concept of "as above, so below."

Similarly, Buddhist teachings emphasize the role of mindful intention, where deep focus and belief help manifest desired outcomes in life. Once we focus our attention and thoughts in one direction we can force the universe to get things done.

Visualization and the Mind-Heart Connection

A. Neuroscience Perspective: Unlocking the Brain's Role in Visualization

i) Reticular Activating System (RAS): The Brain's Gatekeeper of Focus

The Reticular Activating System (RAS) is a network of neurons located in the brainstem that acts as a filter, determining which information is important and worth our attention. Our brain processes massive amounts of data every second, but the RAS ensures that we focus only on what aligns with our goals and priorities.

When we visualize our desired outcomes, we program the RAS to recognize and highlight opportunities that resonate with our goals. For example, if someone visualizes getting a job in a specific industry, they are more likely to notice relevant job postings, networking opportunities, and resources that support that goal. This selective focus enables individuals to take inspired action toward their aspirations.

ii) Mirror Neurons: The Science of Mental Rehearsal

Mirror neurons, specialized brain cells responsible for imitation and empathy, play a crucial role in the visualization process. When we vividly imagine ourselves achieving a goal—such as delivering a confident speech, excelling in a competition, or succeeding in a business venture—mirror neurons fire as if we are physically experiencing the moment.

This process trains the brain to perform imagined scenarios in real life. By visualizing success consistently, individuals prepare their minds to achieve their goals more effectively.

B. Psychological Perspective: Shaping Thought Patterns for Success

i) Cognitive-Behavioral Theory: Changing Thoughts, Changing Outcomes

The Cognitive-Behavioral Theory (CBT) explains that thoughts shape emotions and actions. Negative thinking causes self-doubt, while positive visualization builds strength, motivation, and focus. If a person imagines handling challenges with confidence, they are more likely to stay strong and solve problems in real life. By changing thought patterns, visualization helps create a mindset for success.

ii) Self-Efficacy and Belief: Seeing is Believing

Psychologist Albert Bandura's concept of self-efficacy refers to believing in one's ability to achieve goals. Visualization boosts confidence and strengthens the belief that success is possible, making individuals more likely to take action and reach their dreams.

When people repeatedly visualize themselves accomplishing their goals, they cultivate a sense of certainty that influences their decisions and actions. This belief acts as a self-fulfilling prophecy—those who trust in their abilities are more likely to take proactive steps, persist through challenges, and ultimately achieve their aspirations.

C. Heart Coherence: The Emotional and Physiological Link to Manifestation

i) Heart-Brain Connection: The Science of Intuitive Intelligence

Studies conducted by the Institute of HeartMath highlight the powerful connection between the heart and the brain. The heart has its complex nervous system, often referred to as the "heart brain," which communicates with the brain and influences cognitive function, intuition, and decision-making.

When individuals experience positive emotions such as gratitude, joy, and love, their heart rhythms become more coherent—a state where the heart and brain are in harmony. This coherence enhances creativity, problem-solving skills, and overall well-being, making visualization more effective.

ii) Emotional Guidance: Aligning Thoughts with Feelings

Manifestation is most effective when thoughts and emotions are in alignment. The heart plays a crucial role in guiding the visualization process. When people visualize their goals while experiencing strong, heartfelt emotions—such as the excitement of success or the warmth of gratitude—the brain registers these emotions as real experiences.

This emotional engagement sends powerful signals to the subconscious mind, reinforcing the belief that the desired outcome is already unfolding. The stronger the emotional connection to a visualization, the faster and more effectively the subconscious works to align reality with that vision.

By integrating neuroscience, psychology, and heart coherence principles, visualization becomes a scientifically supported and holistically powerful technique for manifesting success and transforming one's life.

When combined with consistent action and belief, visualization turns dreams into tangible reality, making success achievable.

Ancient Wisdom and the Power of Visualization

A. Vedic Teachings: Tapping into the Universe

Rigveda: Aligning with Cosmic Energy

The Rigveda, one of the oldest Indian scriptures, speaks of the deep connection between the human mind and the universe. It teaches that through focused intent and visualization, one can align with cosmic forces and bring their desires into reality.

Patanjali's Yoga Sutras: The Art of Focus

The Yoga Sutras of Patanjali highlight the importance of Dharana (concentration) and dhyana (meditation) in reaching higher states of awareness. Visualization plays a key role in these practices, helping the mind sharpen its focus and bring clarity to one's aspirations.

B. Hermetic Wisdom: Mind Over Matter

The Kybalion: The Universe Is Mental

The Kybalion, an ancient Hermetic text, introduces the idea that the entire universe is shaped by the mind. This principle, called mentalism, teaches that our thoughts have the power to shape reality—making visualization a direct tool to influence the world around us.

The Emerald Tablet: As Above, So Below

The Emerald Tablet, another key Hermetic text, emphasizes the idea that the mental and physical worlds are interconnected. This ancient wisdom supports the concept of visualization, suggesting that what we hold in our minds can manifest in our lives.

How to Make Visualization More Powerful

A. Be Clear and Specific

The more detailed your vision, the stronger its effect. Instead of saying, "I want success," visualize exactly what success looks like—your career, lifestyle, and achievements. Picture the clothes you're wearing, the place you're in, and the people around you.

Include sounds, smells, and actions to make the vision more

vivid and real. Clarity gives your mind a clear target to aim for. The universe responds faster when your desires are specific and focused.

B. Feel the Emotion

Visualization works best when paired with strong emotions. Feel the joy, excitement, and gratitude as if your dream has already come true. The stronger your emotions, the faster you align with your goal.

Emotion is the fuel that powers your mental images into reality.

Your heart and mind must work together to create a powerful energy flow. When you feel it deeply, your brain believes it's already happening.

This emotional connection speeds up the manifestation process naturally.

C. Make it a Habit

Consistency is key! Practice visualization daily, even if it's just for a few minutes. The brain forms new neural connections through repetition, making your dreams feel more achievable.

Over time, this rewires your subconscious mind to accept your vision as reality. You'll naturally begin to take inspired actions that move you closer to your goals. Morning and bedtime are great times to visualize, as the mind is most relaxed then.

Use calming music or affirmations to boost your focus and emotional connection. You can also write your vision in a journal to make it feel even more real. Reading it daily reinforces belief and keeps your mind centered on your goals. Trust the process, stay patient, and let your imagination lead the way.

D. Add Gratitude to the Process

Be thankful for what you are visualizing as if it has already happened. Gratitude shifts your mindset to abundance, reinforcing positive energy and making manifestation easier. Always be grateful for what you have because the life you are living is someone's dream.

Gratitude opens your heart and aligns you with the frequency of receiving. The more you appreciate, the more the universe gives you to be thankful for. Write down what you're thankful for every day—even small things matter.

This daily habit strengthens your belief and keeps your focus on the positive.

The Science Behind Visualization

A. Sports and Performance Enhancement

Research in sports psychology shows that mentally rehearsing movements activates the same brain regions as physically performing the task, leading to better execution and confidence.

Many elite athletes, from Olympic champions to professional sports players, incorporate mental imagery into their training routines.

By vividly picturing themselves executing perfect techniques, scoring goals, or crossing the finish line first, they enhance muscle memory and refine their skills without physical strain.

Beyond physical performance, visualization strengthens motivation and goal-setting. When athletes imagine themselves standing on the podium, holding a trophy, or breaking a record, their belief in their abilities grows, fueling their determination to achieve those milestones.

The power of visualization extends beyond training; it helps in recovery as well. Injured athletes often use guided imagery to visualize their body's healing, accelerating the rehabilitation process and maintaining a strong mindset during recovery.

From refining techniques to fostering mental toughness, visualization is a proven tool that bridges the gap between preparation and peak performance.

B. Healing Through Visualization

Studies in psychoneuroimmunology suggest that visualizing the body's healing can boost the immune system and improve recovery rates. Patients who imagine themselves getting better often experience faster healing and greater well-being. This mind-body connection is supported by research showing that positive mental imagery can reduce stress, lower inflammation, and enhance the body's natural ability to fight illness.

When individuals practice visualization, they engage in mental exercises where they picture their cells regenerating, wounds closing, or their immune system actively fighting off disease. This process sends signals to the brain, which then communicates with the body, triggering physiological responses that support healing. Studies have shown that cancer patients who use guided imagery alongside medical treatments often report less pain, improved mood, and better overall recovery.

Additionally, visualization has been linked to the placebo effect—where patients experience real improvements in health simply because they believe they are receiving treatment. This highlights the profound influence of the mind on physical health. Athletes, for example, use mental imagery to accelerate injury recovery by imagining their muscles repairing and their bodies regaining strength.

Moreover, practices like meditation, deep breathing, and guided visualization have been found to lower blood pressure, reduce anxiety, and improve sleep—factors that contribute to a stronger immune response. By combining visualization with healthy lifestyle choices, individuals can create an environment that supports both mental and physical well-being.

The power of the mind is undeniable, and when harnessed correctly, it can become a valuable tool in the healing process. Whether recovering from an illness, managing chronic pain, or striving for better overall health, visualization can serve as a powerful complement to medical treatment, fostering hope, resilience, and a positive outlook on recovery.

C. Visualization in Business and Career Growth

Successful entrepreneurs and business leaders visualize their goals before achieving them. Studies show that people who mentally picture themselves achieving career success, meeting financial goals, or leading a company are more likely to turn these visions into reality. By visualizing their achievements, they create a roadmap in their minds, which influences their actions, decisions, and ability to seize opportunities.

When we repeatedly imagine ourselves succeeding, we condition our brains to expect success. This mental rehearsal boosts confidence, sharpens focus, and strengthens the belief that our goals are attainable. Entrepreneurs who use visualization techniques often experience increased motivation, better problem-solving skills, and a stronger ability to overcome obstacles.

Visualization isn't just a wishful-thinking technique; it's an ancient and scientifically-backed tool that can reprogram your mind, align you with your goals, and create real change. It works by activating the brain's reticular activating system (RAS), making us more aware of relevant opportunities that align with our vision. Whether it's preparing for a major business deal, launching a startup, or stepping into a leadership role, visualization helps individuals embody the mindset of success before they physically achieve it.

When practiced with clarity, emotion, and consistency, visualization bridges the gap between thought and reality. The more detailed and emotionally charged the visualization, the more effective it becomes. By imagining the sights, sounds, and feelings associated with success, we send strong signals to our subconscious mind, reinforcing the belief that our dreams are within reach.

Start imagining your dream life today—because what you see in your mind, you can hold in your hands! Your thoughts shape your actions, and your actions shape your reality. See yourself thriving, believe in your vision, and take steps to bring it to life.

Benefits of Visualization

Visualization, often described as watching a movie with closed eyes, taps into the profound capacity of our mind's eye, leveraging the sense of vision to shape our reality. As Sant Kabir wisely said, "Close your eyes. Fall in love. Stay there."

*1. **Sensory Dominance:***

- Among the five senses, vision takes the lead, playing a pivotal role in our perception of the world. However, the magic of visualization lies not in open-eyed observation but in the realm of closed-eye imagination.

*2. **Parade of Mental Imagery:***

- Closing our eyes often unleashes a parade of mental images—memories of friends and family, fears, and fantastical scenarios. Sant Tulsidas beautifully encapsulates this mental landscape,

> *"Closing the eyes and fixing the mind on the Divine brings about the manifestation of the Supreme."*

*3. **Exploring the Art of Visualization:***

- To understand the potency of visualization, one must ponder over the enchanting question: What if we intentionally focus on a specific mental image? Sant

Rajinder Singh Ji Maharaj emphasizes,

"Visualization is a powerful tool to bring us into the present moment."

4. **Comparing Visualization and Affirmations:**

- Drawing an analogy, if visualization is the soccer player in the game of manifestation, affirmations serve as the cheerleaders. In the words of Swami Sivananda,

"Your thoughts and your nature depend on your vision of God. If your vision of God is good, your thoughts and nature will also be good."

5. **Mental Workout and Goal Achievement:**

- Visualization transcends mere positive vibes; it's a mental workout. Sant Maharishi Mahesh Yogi's wisdom resonates here,

"The important thing is this: to be able at any moment to sacrifice what we are for what we could become."

6. **Engaging All Senses:**

- Beyond envisioning success, visualization engages all senses, making it a holistic experience.

Sant Guru Nanak's teachings echo,

"Let your mind be focused on the One, who is beyond the three modes of Maya."

7. **Belief in the Power of Thought:**

- It embodies the belief that positive thoughts pave the way for positive outcomes. As

Mahatma Gandhi profoundly stated,

"A man is but the product of his thoughts. What he thinks, he becomes."

8. **Making Dreams Reality:**

- Whether in personal or professional realms, the act of visualizing transforms dreams into tangible reality. Sant Kabir's timeless verse guides us,

"Whatever you see, is He alone. When you see the world, it is only Him."

In the realm of visualization, closing our eyes becomes a portal to a universe where dreams materialize, guided by the wisdom of spiritual luminaries who remind us that what we envision, we become.

My Story

Now let's talk about a practical tip that I tried and implemented in my life to achieve my next big goal—owning a four-wheeler.

After learning about the power of visualization and vision boards, I decided to put it to the test.

I created my vision board, and the next thing I deeply desired was a car—something I had dreamed about for years.

Every day, 30 minutes before bedtime and 30 minutes after waking up, I followed a simple but powerful routine.

I would sit down, put on meditative music, close my eyes, and imagine myself driving that car.

I didn't just see the car—I felt it. I imagined gripping the steering wheel, feeling the cool breeze from the AC, and hearing the smooth hum of the engine.

I pictured my mother's face glowing with joy as she sat beside me, the confidence in my heart, and the pride of achieving my goal.

I visualized every small detail—the color of the car, the smell of the new leather seats, and even the way the keys felt in my hand.

Once I was done visualizing, I would simply go to sleep, trusting that the universe was aligning everything for me.

Little did I know that this simple daily habit was setting powerful forces into motion, bringing me one step closer to making my dream a reality.

"A reality that was once a dream"

Today, I drive my dream car and feel the same way, as I used to while imagining. Now, you might ask why I am talking about the night and early morning time only, the answer is: that your subconscious mind is in high gear during these periods. Just like me, you can also achieve your dreams.

Let's practically do it now:

- Grab your vision board.
- Sit in a quiet place.
- Put on some calming music.

- Slowly close your eyes and breathe.
- Breath as slow as possible, Inhale...for 7-10 seconds..., Exhale...for 7-10 seconds....
- Focus on your breath & repeat for 1-2 minutes.
- Once your mind is calm, create a story—see yourself as the hero and master of your life, living the dream.
- Dive deep into the emotions until it feels real.

Once you've lived your dream in your mind, it's time to hit the hay. Your mind is in that dream state, and emotions are fresh. As you drift to sleep, imagine your dream life.

The moment between being partially awake and partially asleep is when the subconscious mind is wide awake. It takes your dreams seriously and works to make them real.

Note: Remember, visualization and dreaming alone won't get you everything. They're tools that bring the opportunities, people, ideas, and stepping stones to reach your goal. It's you, only you, who needs to seize those opportunities.

CHAPTER SEVEN

THE TESLA ALIGNMENT METHOD

The Power of Numbers in Manifestation

Numbers have always been important in helping us understand the world. From old spiritual beliefs to today's ways of making dreams come true, some numbers are thought to have special energies that can affect reality.

But the link between numbers and making things happen is mostly based on cultural beliefs, not science. There is no clear proof that seeing the same numbers again and again can change the real world. Still, many people think these numbers help them stay focused, think positively, and set clear intentions.

For a long time, people have used numerology to understand life's patterns. The ancient Egyptians, Greeks, and Chinese believed numbers had a deep connection to the spiritual world. They saw numbers as a way to link the physical and spiritual sides of life. Holy books like the Vedas and the Kabbalah also talk about how numbers help explain the universe.

Even today, people still believe in the power of numbers. One example is the 369 Manifestation Method. This idea became popular because of Nikola Tesla's famous words about 3, 6, and 9 being the key to the universe. In this method, a person repeats their wishes in a set way—three times in the morning, six times in the afternoon, and nine times at night.

The idea behind this method is that repeating something in an organized way while feeling strong emotions can help the mind accept the goal as real. People who practice this say that by focusing on certain numbers and thinking positive thoughts, they can make real changes in their lives.

Also, math is the base of everything in the universe. Every natural event follows several patterns—from the way galaxies spin to the repeating cycles in nature. The Fibonacci sequence, the golden ratio, and special shapes in nature all suggest that numbers play a deep role in shaping reality.

Whether seen as something magical or just a way to train the mind, using numbers to create change still inspires many people. Some see it as a spiritual belief, while others use it to build confidence and develop good habits.

At its heart, the power of numbers in making things happen might come from their ability to improve focus, strengthen belief, and help people feel connected to their goals. Whether through old traditions or modern methods, numbers remain an interesting link between the human mind and the mysteries of life.

The Mystical Significance of Numbers: The Power of 9 in the Universe

Have you ever noticed that many important numbers in shapes, math, and spiritual beliefs add up to 9? This isn't just random; many people think it's a secret clue to how the universe is built.

Number 9 in Math Patterns

A 45-degree angle: $4 + 5 = 9$

A 360-degree circle: $3 + 6 + 0 = 9$

A 180-degree straight angle: $1 + 8 + 0 = 9$

A mala (prayer beads) used for meditation has 108 beads → 1 + 0 + 8 = 9

This repeated appearance of 9 in sacred shapes, number meanings, and spiritual beliefs suggests a deep order in the universe—one that connects both the physical world and the hidden forces beyond it.

The Cosmic Role of Numbers

Old civilizations, from the Egyptians to the Greeks, Hindus, and Mayans, saw numbers as holy. They believed math was not something humans created but something they discovered—a language that the universe itself speaks.

In Hindu beliefs, the number 108 is seen as special, symbolizing the completeness of life. In the same way, Tibetan Buddhist monks repeat their prayers 108 times to connect their energy with higher spiritual levels.

In Pythagorean numerology, the number 9 stands for completion, wisdom, and deep understanding. It shows the end of a full cycle—like the last step before a fresh start.

Many mystical traditions believe that numbers carry vibrations, shaping reality and influencing consciousness. Sacred geometry, which connects shapes and numbers, suggests that patterns like the Fibonacci sequence and the golden ratio reflect the fundamental structure of nature. The ancients saw these patterns in everything—from the spirals of galaxies to the arrangement of leaves on a tree. Even modern scientists have found mathematical principles guiding biological growth, planetary orbits, and even human DNA, reinforcing the idea that numbers are woven into the fabric of existence.

The 369 Connection: Nikola Tesla's Key to the Universe

Nikola Tesla, one of the smartest minds in history, once said:

"If you knew the magnificence of 3, 6, and 9, you would have the key to the universe."

Tesla believed these numbers contained secret patterns of the universe. If you look at multiplication and division cycles, they often lead back to 3, 6, and 9, hinting at a deeper design behind everything.

Some researchers suggest that these numbers form a mathematical blueprint that governs energy flow and frequencies in nature. In vortex mathematics, 3, 6, and 9 are seen as key numbers in an infinite energy loop, unlocking hidden potentials in the way energy moves. Many believe that understanding and applying these numbers could lead to advancements in free energy, spiritual awakening, and a deeper connection with universal forces.

Why Does This Matter for Manifestation?

Knowing these number patterns helps us connect with the universe's energy on purpose. Whether you meditate, imagine your dreams, or pray, the main idea stays the same:

"Where focus goes, energy flows."

By repeating affirmations in a structured number pattern (like the 369 method), we bring our thoughts, feelings, and goals in line with a deeper rhythm of the universe—one that mystics, scientists, and spiritual seekers have recognized for ages.

But why 3, 6, and 9 specifically? The answer lies in ancient wisdom, mathematical principles, and energetic vibrations that influence reality.

The Power of Three (3): In history, the number 3 represents creation, balance, and divine order. Many religious texts mention a trinity—Father, Son, and Holy Spirit in Christianity, or Brahma, Vishnu, and Shiva in Hinduism. Manifestation begins with thought (idea), word (expression), and action (execution), forming the sacred triangle of creation.

The Energy of Six (6): In numerology, 6 is the number of harmony, nurturing, and manifestation. It acts as a bridge between the material and spiritual realms, symbolizing balance. Tesla suggested that 6 is a key frequency in the natural cycles of energy, representing movement and transformation. When used in manifestation, it aligns our desires with the flow of the universe, ensuring that what we seek is received in divine timing.

The Completion of Nine (9): The number 9 represents completion, enlightenment, and the highest level of consciousness. In ancient teachings, 9 is seen as the final step before a new beginning, symbolizing the full cycle of creation. When we use 9 in manifestation techniques, we reinforce our desires with universal wisdom, allowing them to materialize fully.

Science and the 369 Manifestation Code

Vortex Mathematics: This branch of math shows that numbers 3, 6, and 9 create a unique energy pattern that doesn't fit into the normal doubling sequence (e.g., 1, 2, 4, 8, 16, 32). Instead, they hold a separate key to the universe's infinite energy cycles.

Brainwave Influence: Studies suggest that repeating affirmations and meditations in structured sequences affects gamma brain waves, boosting creativity and problem-solving skills—essential for manifesting goals.

Quantum Physics & Frequency Alignment: Everything in the universe vibrates at a frequency, and manifestation is about matching our thoughts to the desired outcome's frequency. Tesla believed 369 numbers influence frequency patterns, helping shift thoughts from the imagination stage to reality.

By using the 369 method—writing or saying an intention 3 times in the morning, 6 times in the afternoon, and 9 times at night—we strengthen the connection between our desires and the universe's natural flow. This repeated focus embeds the idea deeply into the subconscious mind, making it more likely to manifest in the physical world.

Final Thought

The 369 pattern is not just a random sequence—it is a formula rooted in ancient knowledge, mathematics, and energy principles. Whether used in spiritual rituals, meditation, or quantum manifestation techniques, these numbers help us harness universal forces to create the life we desire.

The Numerology of 3, 6, and 9

- According to Numerology:
- 3 stands for creativity, self-expression, and the power to communicate.
- 6 is linked to balance, harmony, and caring energy.
- 9 represents spiritual wisdom, higher awareness, and a deep connection to the universe.
- The 369 manifestation method uses the strength of these numbers to boost intentions and turn desires into reality.

Step-by-Step Guide to the 369 Manifestation Technique

Step 1: Be Clear About What You Want

Know exactly what you wish for. Instead of saying, "I want financial success," write:

"Thank you for giving me xxxxxxx amount of money."

Step 2: Write Your Desire in the Present Tense

Always state your wish as if it is already real. This helps train your mind to believe in it and take action.

For example, instead of writing "I want to be healthy," write "I am healthy and full of energy."

The present tense sends a clear message to your subconscious that this is your current reality, not a distant dream.

This shift in language creates a stronger emotional connection and builds confidence in your vision.

Over time, your thoughts and behavior begin to align with

the reality you've written down.

Step 3: Break It Down into 3 Sentences

Turn your affirmation into three strong, clear statements that reflect your goal, the process, and the result. This structure helps your mind absorb and believe the message more deeply. Begin with gratitude, follow with flow, and end with fulfillment.

Example:

I am truly grateful for my growing financial success.
Money flows to me effortlessly through multiple sources.
I now live a secure and abundant life filled with prosperity.

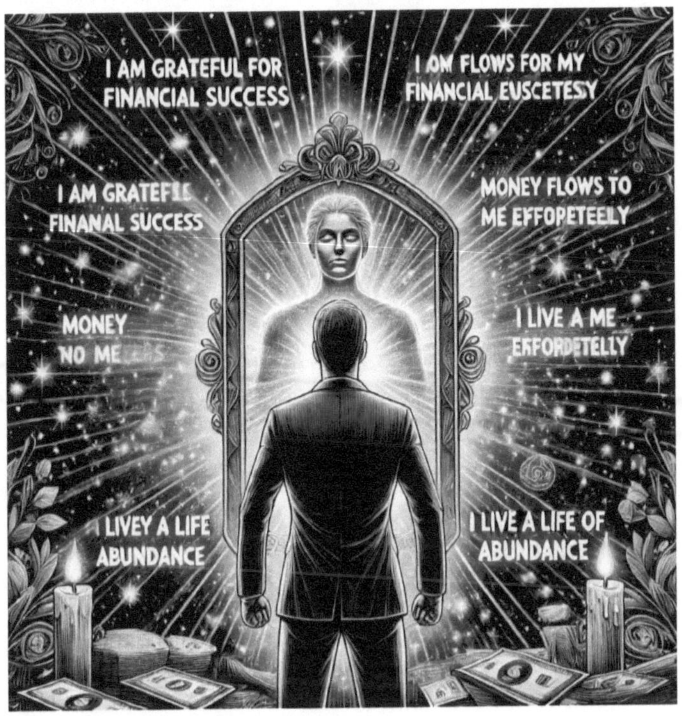

Step 4: Repeat It 6 Times

Repeating something again and again helps train your mind to believe it. Say or write each of your three sentences six times to make your goal stronger in your thoughts. The more you repeat it, the deeper it becomes part of your mind.

Each time you say or write your affirmation, imagine it happening with full feelings. Feel happy, excited, or grateful, as if you already have what you want. This isn't just about saying words—it's about making your mind truly believe your goal is real.

Think of it like planting a seed in your mind. Every time you repeat your affirmation, you water that seed, helping it grow into reality. Over time, this focus shapes your thoughts, choices, and actions to match your dreams.

For best results, use all your senses—say the words out loud, picture them in your mind, and write them with purpose. The more real it feels, the stronger the effect.

Stay consistent, and soon, you'll see small changes in your thinking, energy, and chances that bring you closer to your goal.

Step 5: Summarize in 9 Affirmations

Create nine short and powerful affirmations that support your goal. Example:

- I am financially abundant.
- I attract prosperity every day.
- I attract only positive things in life.
- Opportunities come to me easily.
- Money flows to me naturally.
- I make smart financial choices.
- Success is my right.
- My income keeps growing.

- I welcome wealth and new chances.
- Abundance is all around me.

These short affirmations help reinforce your belief and keep your mind focused on success.

Step 6: Repeat the Process Daily

Consistency is key. Many people follow this schedule:

Morning – Write your goal 3 times

Afternoon – Write your goal 6 times

Night – Write your goal 9 times

"Repetition is the key"

Step 7: Keep a Positive Mindset

Your mindset is the base of successful manifestation. Stay away from doubt and negativity, as they can weaken the energy you are sending toward your dreams. If negative thoughts come up—like "This isn't working" or "I don't deserve this"—replace them right away with positive affirmations like:

"Everything is happening perfectly for me."
"I deserve all my dreams and desires."

Belief is key. If you don't truly believe in your goal, your mind may resist it. Build trust in the process by remembering past successes, even small ones. Every little win proves that you can make things happen.

This shifts your energy and helps you stay connected to abundance. Your thoughts shape your energy, and your energy shapes your reality.

Speak kindly to yourself—your words become instructions to the universe. Visualize your dreams clearly, and feel the emotions as if they've already come true.

Gratitude multiplies manifestation—be thankful for what you have and what's on the way.

Let go of how and when; focus on trust, not control.

Surround yourself with people and things that uplift your spirit. The more aligned you are with your desires, the faster they flow into your life.

Surround Yourself with Positivity

Spend time with people who support and inspire you. Read books, listen to affirmations, or watch motivational videos that strengthen your belief in the power of your thoughts.

If you ever feel discouraged, look at your vision board or re-read your affirmations. Remind yourself why you started this journey. Your dreams are real, and every step forward—no matter how small—brings you closer to them.

Stay patient and trust the process. Just like a seed takes time to grow into a tree, your manifestations need time to become real. Keep believing, and soon, you'll see your dreams come true.

Enhancing the 369 Manifestation Method

Have a Clear Goal – If you want a car, be specific about the brand, color, and model.

Write in Present Tense – Imagine and feel as if you already own it.

Engage Your Emotions – Picture the happiness of achieving it.

Visualize Daily – Spend a few minutes seeing your dream as real in your mind.

Use a Vision Board – Add pictures that represent your goals and review them often.

Believe Deeply – Trust that the universe is already working to bring your dream to you.

Daily Routine Example:

Morning: Wake up → Stretch → Meditate → Write affirmations 3 times

Afternoon: Meditate → Write affirmations 6 times

Night: Meditate → Write affirmations 9 times

Following this routine keeps your focus strong and helps you align your energy with your desires.

My Personal Experience

At first, this method didn't work for me—I was just writing affirmations without feeling them. It felt like a task instead of a powerful practice.

Then, I tried something new—I chanted "Om" before writing my affirmations. This helped calm my mind and brought me into the present moment. When I started writing again, I felt like I was truly living my dream. It wasn't just words on paper anymore—it became a real experience.

The emotions felt stronger, and my manifestation became more powerful. Instead of just hoping for my desires, I felt joy, gratitude, and confidence—as if they had already come true.

This small shift changed everything. I learned that visualization and affirmations are not just about repeating words—they are about feeling your dreams as if they are already real.

So, try this method with an open heart. You might need to adjust it based on what feels right for you. Experiment with meditation, breathing exercises, or soft music before writing your affirmations.

The secret is to use all your senses and emotions to make your manifestation more real.

"Stay tuned! In the next chapter, we'll explore even more ways to unlock your full potential!"

CHAPTER EIGHT

AFFIRMATION AMPLIFICATION

The 555 Manifestation Technique: A Simple Yet Powerful Way to Change Your Life

Have you ever wished for a magic method that could help turn your dreams into reality? Something that makes success, happiness, and abundance come into your life easily? The 555 Manifestation Technique might be exactly what you need!

This method is based on ancient wisdom and numerology and gives you a clear and simple way to manifest your desires. By understanding the power of numbers and using repetition, you can train your mind to attract what you truly want.

Let's Explore the 555 Manifestation Technique: Its Meaning and How to Use It

What is Numerology and Why is 555 Special?

Numbers have shaped our world for centuries. From ancient times to modern science, they help us understand patterns, energy, and even our journeys.

Different cultures see numbers as having deep meanings:

Hinduism – The Vedas describe numbers as keys to understanding the universe. Many sacred symbols, like yantras, use specific numbers to represent cosmic energy.

Kabbalah (Jewish Mysticism) – The Tree of Life has ten spheres, each connected to a divine number that links to spiritual energy.

Chinese Numerology – The I Ching, one of the oldest books in history, gives special meanings to numbers to predict the future.

Among all numbers, five is unique because it represents change, growth, and transformation. It helps break old patterns and opens the door to new beginnings.

Why 555?

In numerology:

Three fives together (555) increase the power of change.

It is a sign of a big shift in life.

It represents a doorway to new opportunities.

This is why the 555 Manifestation Technique uses repetition and visualization to bring real change into your life.

How to Use the 55x5 Method in 5 Simple Steps

The 55x5 method is a simple way to bring your desires into reality. You only need five days and 55 repetitions of a strong affirmation each day. Here's how to do it:

Step 1: Be Clear About What You Want

The universe works best with clear instructions. Instead of saying, "I want to be rich," say:

"I am financially free, and money flows to me easily."

Instead of saying, "I want love," say:

"I am in a loving and fulfilling relationship with my perfect partner."

Be specific, and make sure your desire feels exciting and real.

Step 2: Create a Powerful Affirmation

Affirmations declare your goal as if it has already happened.

A strong affirmation should be:

Positive (Avoid words like "don't" or "not.")

Present tense (Write as if it's happening now.)

Emotionally charged (Make it something you truly feel.)

For example:

"I am so happy and grateful that I have my dream job, earning $10,000 a month, doing what I love."

Step 3: Write It Down 55 Times a Day for 5 Days

Take a notebook and write your affirmation 55 times each day for five days.

Why writing? Writing trains your subconscious mind. The more you repeat something, the more your brain believes it to be true.

Step 4: Feel It While You Write

As you write, imagine yourself already living that reality.

How does it feel?

What does your life look like?

What emotions come up?

Picture yourself driving that dream car, signing that business deal, or living in that dream home. The stronger your emotions, the faster your manifestation works. Feel the pride, the joy, and the peace that come with achieving your dream. Let those emotions fill your heart and guide your actions each day.

Step 5: Let Go and Trust the Process
Once you finish your five days, release any doubts and allow the universe to do its work.

Many people expect instant results, but manifestation requires faith and patience. Trust that your desire is already on its way.

Why Does the Number 5 Hold So Much Power?

The number five is known as a symbol of transformation in many cultures. Here's why:

1. The Power of the Pentagram (Five-Pointed Star)
In spiritual teachings, the pentagram represents balance:

- Earth – Stability
- Water – Emotion
- Fire – Passion
- Air – Intellect
- Spirit – Connection to the higher self

By bringing these elements together, we create harmony and alignment—which is exactly what manifestation is about.

2. Sacred Geometry and the Number 5
Ancient sacred geometry, like the Flower of Life, is based on the number five. This pattern is believed to contain the blueprint of creation, making five several divine powers.

3. 555 as a Sign of Big Change
Seeing 555 is often a message that a major transformation is coming. Many believe it is a sign that

you are on the right path and should welcome new opportunities into your life.

The Science Behind the 555 Technique

Some people may wonder—does this work? Here's how science backs it up:

1. The Power of Repetition

Studies in neuroscience show that when we repeat something often, it creates new pathways in the brain. This means:

The more we affirm something, the more our brain accepts it as true.

We start acting in ways that bring us closer to our goal because our subconscious mind believes it is possible.

2. The Law of Attraction

The Law of Attraction states that what we focus on, we attract. This means: If you focus on success, you will bring more success into your life. If you focus on negativity, you will attract more negative experiences.

By writing affirmations, you keep your mind focused on what you want instead of what you lack.

Your thoughts act like magnets—what you constantly think about begins to shape your reality. Gratitude, positive thinking, and clear intentions boost this effect even more.

Visualization and belief are tools that help you stay in the vibration of your desires. When your energy matches your goals, the universe responds accordingly. Stay consistent, trust the process, and watch your life slowly reflect your inner focus.

3. The Placebo Effect

Have you heard of the placebo effect? It happens when people heal just because they believe they are receiving medicine—even when they are not.This shows how belief alone can create real changes, proving that what the mind accepts, the body follows.

Doctors have seen patients recover with sugar pills, simply because they believed they were being treated.This proves that belief isn't just emotional—it can trigger real physical reactions.The brain releases chemicals based on belief, affecting healing, energy, and mood.

It shows the deep link between mind and body and how powerful thoughts truly are. This is why positive visualization, trust, and faith can speed up healing and personal growth. Believing in your transformation is often the first step to making it real.

This proves that **belief alone can create real change in the body and mind.**

The 555 technique works similarly—it reprograms your belief system, helping you align with your desires.

By writing your affirmation 55 times for 5 days, you send a clear message to your subconscious.

This repetition strengthens your focus and builds the energy needed to attract what you want.

Does the 555 Method Work for Everyone?

Like All Manifestation Techniques, the 555 Method Needs Belief and Consistency

Some people see results quickly, while for others, it takes time.

Common Challenges:

Writing without emotion – Just writing words will not work. You need to feel them.

Doubting the process – If you don't believe it will work, it won't.

Expecting instant results – The universe works at its own pace. Trust the process.

Success Stories

Many people have used the 555 Manifestation Technique to:

Get job offers and promotions

Attract new relationships

Manifest unexpected money

Create positive life changes

The key to success is faith, patience, and action.

Final Thoughts: Manifest Your Dream Life

The 555 Manifestation Technique is a simple yet powerful way to attract the life you want. It combines ancient wisdom, numerology, and modern psychology to help train your mind for success.

If you are ready to change your life, commit to trying this method for five days.

Write. Feel. Believe. Manifest.

The universe is always listening—what will you ask for?

CHAPTER NINE

AQUARIUS ALCHEMY

Introduction

The desire to control natural elements and unlock their transformative power has been a goal across cultures and history. Among many techniques, the Water Manifestation Technique stands out as a unique method that blends ancient wisdom with modern goals.

In this guide, we will explore the origins, steps, and references to water manifestation in ancient scriptures, showing proof of its existence and effectiveness.

Water: The Element of Creation and Transformation

Water, often called the source of life, has always been linked to purification, renewal, and creation. From sacred books to spiritual practices, civilizations have recognized its power to absorb intentions and amplify energy.

Ancient scholars and spiritual leaders believed that water serves as a bridge between thought and reality, turning desires into real experiences.

The steady movement of water reflects the constant flow of energy, making it a perfect tool for manifestation practices. When water is charged with focused intent, it helps the subconscious mind align with conscious goals, strengthening the power of belief. This technique has been mentioned in Vedic traditions, Taoist teachings, and indigenous rituals, showing its deep-rooted history across cultures.

Scientific studies on water memory and vibrational frequencies also support the idea that water absorbs and responds to energy. Researchers like Dr. Masaru Emoto have studied how water molecules change based on emotions, words, and intentions, proving a strong link between thoughts and the physical world.

By learning and using the Water Manifestation Technique, people can apply this ancient wisdom to change their reality, attract abundance, and manifest their deepest desires.

Origins of Water Manifestation Technique

The Water Manifestation Technique has its roots in ancient civilizations, where natural elements were seen as both spiritual and powerful forces shaping reality.

This technique became well-known through mysticism, spirituality, and practical uses, based on the belief that water, as a symbol of fluidity and life, has special manifesting abilities.

Taoist Philosophy and the Tao Te Ching

One of the earliest references to water's transformative power is found in Taoism. The Tao Te Ching, written by Lao Tzu, describes water's ability to flow effortlessly and adapt, making it a perfect example of the path of least resistance—a key idea in the Water Manifestation Technique.

Vedic Scriptures in Hinduism

In Hindu traditions, water is considered sacred and is often used to carry prayers and divine intentions into the universe. For centuries, mantras have been chanted over water to attract prosperity, healing, and spiritual growth.

Sacred Water Rituals in Ancient Egypt

Ancient Egyptian texts also show the sacred nature of water, linking it to rebirth and renewal. The Nile River, seen as a divine life force, was central to many ceremonies where water was blessed and infused with intentions to attract abundance and transformation.

These traditions reveal how water has been used across cultures as a tool for manifestation, healing, and spiritual connection.

Water as a Sacred Vessel in Spiritual Traditions

In indigenous traditions, water was believed to carry the wisdom of ancestors, acting as a link between the spiritual world and those seeking guidance. Shamans and healers used water in rituals to cleanse energies and make visions real.

Even in early Christian and Islamic traditions, water was connected to purification and divine intervention, strengthening the belief that it serves as a bridge between the physical and spiritual worlds.

From these traditions, it is clear that water has always been seen as more than just an element—it is a tool for transformation, capable of holding, absorbing, and passing on human intentions.

By understanding its historical and spiritual importance, we see why the Water Manifestation Technique has survived across generations, keeping its core power of shaping reality through intention.

The Water Manifestation Technique: A Simple Guide

Water is a powerful element that absorbs energy and intention. By using it with awareness, you can bring your desires to life. This method helps align your thoughts, energy, and goals with the natural flow of the universe.

Step 1: Set Your Intention Clearly

Decide what you want to manifest—health, success, love, or happiness.

Focus your thoughts and emotions on this goal. The clearer your intention, the stronger the energy.

Step 2: Connect with Water's Energy

If possible, sit near a river, lake, or ocean to feel the power of water.

If you are at home, you can still use water—your mind and body are the true tools of manifestation.

Step 3: The Simple Water Ritual (Do This at Home!)

Take a few deep breaths and meditate for 5–10 minutes to calm your mind.

Imagine your dream coming true—see it, feel it, and believe it as if it is already real.

Hold a glass of water close to your mouth and speak your affirmations into it (for example, "I am happy. I am healthy.").

Place the water in a sacred space (like an altar or bedside) for at least an hour before drinking it.

This practice infuses the water with your intention, allowing your body and mind to absorb the energy and make your desire a reality.

4. The Paper & Water Manifestation Method

If you prefer writing, this method is a great way to combine words, water, and visualization to strengthen your manifestation.

Take a piece of paper and write your desires in the present tense, as if they are already happening.

Avoid negative words—focus only on what you want.

Fill a glass with water (glass is best because it is a pure material).

Rub your hands together to build energy, then hold the glass while visualizing your dream as real.

Read your affirmations aloud or silently, focusing on the water.

Once you feel fully connected, drink the water, allowing the energy to flow through you.

5. Sacred Symbols & Rituals

You can add extra power to your practice by using symbols and tools:

Draw sacred symbols like geometric patterns near your water.

Use crystals around the water to amplify energy.

Keep the water overnight and take small sips throughout the day to keep your intention strong.

6. Trust & Let Go

Once you have set your intention and charged the water, release any attachment to the outcome.

Trust that the universe will bring what is meant for you at the right time.

Stay open to opportunities—manifestations sometimes appear in unexpected ways.

Final Thought

It doesn't matter whether you do this in the morning, at night, or throughout the day—the key is belief.

When you infuse water with intention and drink it, you align your body and mind with your desires.

Try this method and watch how your reality begins to change!

CHAPTER TEN

BREAKING THE CHAINS

Arjun's Belief Rebirth

In the lively town of Jaipur, India, between the busy streets and the echoing sounds of the Hawa Mahal, lived a young boy named Arjun. He was a curious and bright child, always fascinated by the world around him.

However, growing up in a traditional Indian family, he often heard negative comments about his abilities.

Arjun's parents, shaped by society's expectations and their own upbringing, unknowingly filled his mind with self-doubt.

"You're not as smart as your cousin," they would say, comparing him to a relative who excelled in school.

"You need to work harder if you want to achieve anything in life," they would warn, not realizing they were planting negative beliefs in his young mind.

As Arjun moved through the challenges of school, he carried the burden of these negative words on his shoulders. No matter how much he tried, he couldn't shake the feeling that he wasn't good enough.

His confidence faded, and the once curious and fearless child began doubting his own abilities.

It was during a school science fair that Arjun's negative thoughts peaked.

As he excitedly presented his project on renewable energy, a classmate mocked him, saying, "You think you can impress anyone with this? You're just a mediocre student."

The words hit him hard, reinforcing every doubt and fear he had been carrying for years.

"Words spoken to a child become the inner voice guiding their future."

Curious, Arjun flipped through its worn-out pages, feeling a strange sense of connection to its words. The book spoke about how thoughts shape reality, how beliefs can be changed, and how the mind is the key to success.

For the first time, he realized that the negative beliefs he had carried for years were not his own—they were simply planted ideas from others.

Determined to change, Arjun devoured the book, practicing the exercises it suggested. He began repeating positive affirmations, visualizing success, and challenging the doubts that had once held him back.

With each passing day, he felt a shift in his mindset. The voice of self-doubt grew quieter, replaced by a newfound belief in himself.

He noticed small changes at first—more confidence in conversations, a sense of calm in stressful moments. Doors that once seemed closed slowly began to open, as if the world was responding to his inner transformation.
He started journaling his thoughts, tracking his progress, and celebrating every little victory. The more he believed, the more aligned his actions became with his dreams.

Challenges still came, but he faced them with strength instead of fear. He no longer felt like a victim of his circumstances—instead, he felt like the creator of his path.

His relationships improved, his goals became clearer, and his days felt more purposeful. Arjun realized that real change doesn't happen overnight, but with daily effort, it becomes inevitable.

That old book, once forgotten on a dusty shelf, had sparked a light within him. And from that moment on, he knew—his story was his to write.

"Sometimes, the greatest discoveries begin in the quiet corners of a bookstore."

Dr. Meera Kapoor, the author, explained how childhood programming—the beliefs and ideas absorbed at a young age—shaped a person's future.

As Arjun read, he realized he wasn't alone.

Dr. Kapoor stressed the importance of reprogramming the mind—a conscious effort to challenge and replace negative thoughts with positive affirmations.

For the first time, Arjun saw a way forward. He wasn't stuck in mediocrity—he could rewrite his own story.

"Your past programming doesn't define you; your ability to rewrite it does."

Inspired by Dr. Kapoor's words, Arjun set out on a journey of self-discovery and transformation. He began by recognizing the negative thoughts that had troubled him for years.

For every doubtful belief, he replaced it with a positive affirmation:

"I am intelligent."

"I am capable."

"I deserve success."

With time and dedication, his mindset began to change. His grades improved, and his love for learning grew stronger.

He stepped out of his comfort zone, joining extracurricular activities and discovering hidden talents he never knew he had. The once uncertain boy evolved into a confident young man, ready to embrace the endless opportunities that life had to offer.

He reached out to Dr. Meera, and both started a mission to transform others' lives. Their mission took them across India, spreading the message of mental reprogramming and teaching people how to take control of their destinies.

"Breaking free from negativity isn't about forgetting your past; it's about reclaiming your power."

Arjun's Legacy of Transformation

Arjun's story became a guiding light for many, proving that with determination and the right mindset, anyone could break free from childhood limitations and reshape their future.

The once-overlooked boy from Jaipur had become a symbol of hope, showing others that self-belief could triumph over negativity.

As the sun set behind the Hawa Mahal, casting its warm glow over the city, Arjun stood tall—a reminder that confidence and persistence could rewrite any story.

The streets of Jaipur echoed with whispers of change, as people across the country embarked on their own journeys of mental reprogramming and positive transformation.

My Story: A Journey from Self-Doubt to Confidence

There was a time in my life when all I wanted was to spread happiness. Even the slightest frown on someone's face could affect my entire day. I constantly searched for ways to make others smile, turning to friends like Harsh, Aashish, and my sister for advice on self-improvement.

I carefully gathered the best lessons and worked on becoming better every single day.

Then, one day, I met Ankush. During our conversation, I unintentionally said something hurtful. Though I apologized immediately, I couldn't stop thinking about it afterward. I kept wondering how to fix things and avoid similar mistakes in the future.

A Wake-Up Call

A few days later, I resumed my habit of asking for improvement suggestions—this time from Aashish, my sister, and even Ankush. To my surprise, Ankush focused on that one mistake, making me realize how much I was depending on others' opinions.

This led me to call my friend "Harsh", hoping for clarity. But his response shook me.

He asked, "Are you trying to be a God?" He reminded me that humans make mistakes and that perfection is impossible. His words hit me hard, forcing me to rethink my endless pursuit of flawlessness.

Still confused, I reached out to my friend "Dimple", who gave me an insight that changed everything.

She urged me to stop seeking external approval, emphasizing that nobody is perfect—not me, not anyone else.

Then, she acknowledged something no one had ever mentioned before—the weight of responsibilities I had carried since my father's passing in 2005.

For the first time, someone truly recognized my struggles. Her words had a deep impact, helping me see my worth in a way I never had before.

The Power of Self-Belief

From that day forward, Dimple's wisdom transformed my life. I stopped doubting myself, faced challenges with confidence, and achieved milestones I once thought impossible.

I realized that, just like Arjun from the ancient tales, I had the power to shape my destiny.

No longer did I allow self-doubt to hold me back. With faith and determination, I tackled life's challenges head-on, achieving success with the grace of a higher power.

This experience taught me one of life's most important lessons—the impact of positive suggestions and self-belief.

You Can Rewrite Your Story Too

Just like Arjun and just like me, you too have the power to take control of your life and shape your destiny.

Make a promise to yourself: Face challenges with confidence. Believe in your abilities. Ignore the doubters.

Every single day, remind yourself: "I CAN DO IT."

Stay focused on your dreams, and one day, you will be living the life you once imagined. And when that day comes, those who once doubted you will be cheering for your success.

CHAPTER ELEVEN

THE ESSENCE OF FOCUS

The Power of Focus: Unlocking Your True Potential

Focus, though simple in concept, holds the key to greatness. In today's world, where distractions are everywhere, mastering focus is essential for personal growth and success.

This exploration looks at the nature of focus, how to develop it, and how distractions impact our lives. We will also draw wisdom from ancient philosophies, which offer timeless insights into the miracles of focus.

Why Focus Matters?

Clarity and Direction – When we focus, we see things more clearly, allowing us to move in the right direction.

Turning the Ordinary into the Extraordinary – Simple tasks become powerful achievements when done with full attention.

Resilience and Calmness – Focus helps us handle challenges with precision and peace of mind.

Purposeful Action – By channeling our focus, we align our intentions with meaningful actions, leading to real change.

Mastering focus is the gateway to success, allowing us to achieve more, think deeply, and transform our lives. Ultimately, cultivating focus empowers us to live intentionally, fulfilling our deepest aspirations.

Understanding Focus

Focus is the deliberate mental effort directed toward a specific task, goal, or thought. It involves channeling attention and energy while eliminating distractions to achieve a desired result.

True focus requires mental discipline and emotional control, leading to a heightened state of awareness and efficiency.

How to Achieve Focus

1. **Understanding Priorities:** To stay focused, first identify and prioritize your goals. Clear objectives act as a roadmap, directing your energy and attention toward what truly matters.

2. **Practicing mindfulness:** Techniques like meditation and mindfulness train the mind to stay present and resist distractions. By improving awareness, mindfulness helps enhance focus and reduce mental clutter.

3. **Structured Planning:** Breaking down big tasks into smaller, manageable steps prevents feeling overwhelmed. A clear plan keeps attention centered, improving productivity and efficiency.

4. **Eliminating Distractions:** A distraction-free environment is crucial for deep focus. Turn off notifications, declutter your workspace, and set clear boundaries to protect your concentration.

The Dangerous Impact of Distractions

Distractions, in all their forms, act as silent destroyers of focus. They drain mental energy, weaken decision-making, and lower productivity. Without strong focus we will only be wandering generality and won't be able to accomplish what we actually desire.

In today's world, where notifications, multitasking, and endless information fight for our attention, staying focused has become harder than ever.

How Technology Contributes to Distractions

Technology—especially smartphones and constant internet access—has changed the way we work and live. Endless notifications from apps, emails, social media, and news constantly interrupt our focus. Instead of deep concentration, our attention becomes scattered, making it harder to complete tasks with full effort and quality.

The result is less meaningful work, lower productivity, and a weakened ability to stay in the moment. Even short glances at a screen can break the flow of thought and delay mental recovery. The habit of checking devices frequently rewires the brain to crave constant stimulation.

Multitasking, encouraged by digital tools, often reduces overall effectiveness. People spend more time reacting than creating, trapped in a loop of shallow tasks. This digital noise prevents us from entering states of deep work or creative flow. Without boundaries, technology shifts from being helpful to being mentally draining.

The Psychological Toll of Constant Distractions

Repeated distractions cause stress, anxiety, and eventually burnout. Each interruption forces the brain to switch tasks, using up its mental energy. Over time, this leads to less clarity, reduced creativity, and poor memory retention.

The brain, overloaded with constant input, struggles to process and retain important information. The result is a feeling of mental exhaustion, making it harder to perform at our best. To protect our focus and well-being, we must learn to control distractions and create an environment that allows deep, meaningful work.

The Myth of Multitasking

Many people believe multitasking makes them more productive, but in reality, it's a myth.

Our brains are not wired to handle multiple tasks at the same time efficiently. What we think of as multitasking is rapid task-switching, where the brain jumps back and forth between different activities.

This constant shifting reduces focus, increases mistakes, and slows down overall performance.

Why Multitasking Slows You Down?

- Constant Switching Wastes Time
- Every time we shift focus, the brain needs time to refocus.
- These small delays add up, slowing down overall productivity.
- Disrupts Concentration
- Switching between tasks breaks deep focus, making it harder to complete anything efficiently.
- Leads to More Mistakes
- The more we divide attention, the more errors creep in.
- Accuracy suffers because the brain is not fully engaged in any one task.
- Causes Mental Fatigue
- Repeatedly shifting focus tires the brain.
- This results in lower energy levels, slower thinking, and reduced creativity.
- The Reality: Single-Tasking is More Effective
- Instead of multitasking, focus on one task at a time. This allows for:
- Deeper concentration
- Higher quality work
- Faster completion
- Fewer mistakes

By embracing single-tasking, you work smarter, not harder, achieving better results in less time.

Ancient Philosophies on Focus

Throughout history, ancient philosophies have emphasized the power of focus and attention as a key to clarity, resilience, and success.

Stoicism: Focus on What You Can Control

Originating in Greece and Rome, Stoicism was practiced by great thinkers like Seneca, Epictetus, and Marcus Aurelius.

At its core, Stoicism teaches that:

"Inner calm and strength come from self-discipline."
We should focus only on what we can control—our thoughts, actions, and attitudes. Detaching from external distractions (like other people's opinions, luck, or unexpected events) brings clarity and resilience. By directing energy inward and practicing emotional discipline, Stoics achieved a clear mind and steady focus, even in difficult situations.

Zen Buddhism: Mindfulness and Single-Tasking

Rooted in East Asia, Zen Buddhism teaches the art of mindfulness and being fully present. One of its key principles is "Zanshin"—a state of complete awareness and focus. Zanshin encourages full dedication to a single activity, performed with complete attention and care.

This idea aligns with modern single-tasking, proving that true efficiency and fulfillment come when we avoid distractions and focus entirely on the task at hand. By practicing mindfulness, Zen teachings help develop deep concentration and awareness in all aspects of life.

Vedanta Philosophy: The Power of Concentration

In Indian philosophy, Vedanta teaches that focused concentration—known as "Dharana"—is an essential step toward mental clarity and self-awareness. Dharana involves fixing the mind on one thought, object, or goal, blocking out distractions.

Regular practice of deep concentration sharpens the mind, enhances clarity, and prepares individuals for deeper meditation and self-realization. According to Vedanta, mastering concentration not only improves mental discipline but also leads to inner wisdom, spiritual growth, and personal success.

Key Takeaways from Ancient Wisdom

- Stoicism – Focus only on what you can control, and ignore distractions.
- Zen Buddhism – Be fully present in everything you do, one task at a time.
- Vedanta – Train your mind through deep concentration to unlock greater clarity and wisdom.

These timeless philosophies prove that focus is not just a modern productivity tool—it is a fundamental key to self-mastery and success.

"Timeless Wisdom: Stoicism, Zen, and Vedanta United in Mindful Focus"

Ancient Wisdom Meets Modern Science: The Neuroscience and Psychology of Focus

Ancient traditions have long emphasized the power of focus, and today, modern science is proving why these practices work. Advances in neuroscience and cognitive psychology provide scientific validation for the principles of single-tasking, mindfulness, and deep concentration.

Neuroscientific Insights: How Focus Shapes the Brain

Modern neuroscience has confirmed that meditation, mindfulness, and focused attention lead to measurable changes in brain structure and function.

Studies show that regular meditation increases gray matter density in key areas of the brain, such as:

- Prefrontal Cortex – Responsible for focus, decision-making, and self-control.
- Hippocampus – Plays a crucial role in memory and learning.

These findings reveal that ancient practices do more than just relax the mind—they physically reshape and strengthen the brain.

Improved brain function leads to sharper attention, stronger memory, and better emotional regulation. Focused attention also strengthens neural pathways, making concentration easier over time.

Even a few minutes of daily mindfulness can create long-term benefits for mental clarity.

In other words, the mental discipline taught in Stoicism, Zen Buddhism, and Vedanta has a direct, lasting impact on cognitive performance and brain health.

Cognitive Psychology: Why Single-Tasking Works

Modern psychology also supports the principles of ancient wisdom, especially in the area of Cognitive Load Theory. According to this theory, the human brain has limited cognitive resources. When we try to multitask, we overload our brains, leading to poor decision-making, slower thinking, and increased mistakes.

Ancient traditions have always taught the power of focusing on one task at a time, and now, science confirms that deep, uninterrupted focus leads to:

- Better learning and memory
- Clearer thinking and faster decision-making
- More efficient problem-solving

It also reduces stress and improves emotional regulation over time. Focused attention allows us to enter "flow states," where we perform at our best. This harmony between ancient practices and modern research is no coincidence. It shows that the human mind thrives when given clarity, space, and purpose.

Both ancient wisdom and modern science agree—that single-tasking, mindfulness, and intentional focus are the keys to optimal cognitive performance and productivity. By applying these time-tested and scientifically proven strategies, we can train our minds, boost mental clarity, and unlock our full potential.

Productivity and Deep Work: The Power of Uninterrupted Focus

In today's world, where constant distractions make it difficult to concentrate, true productivity has become a challenge. To counter this, Cal Newport, a well-known author and productivity expert, introduced the concept of Deep Work—a method of working with complete focus to produce high-quality results.

What is Deep Work?

Deep work is the practice of fully engaging in a task without interruptions, allowing the mind to function at its highest level. It involves:

- Eliminating distractions – No notifications, no multitasking, no interruptions.
- Dedicating uninterrupted time – Setting aside long, focused work sessions.
- Engaging in mentally demanding tasks – Working on projects that require deep thinking and creativity.

When individuals practice deep work, they produce extraordinary results with greater efficiency and less stress.

Ancient Wisdom and Deep Work

This modern productivity method aligns closely with ancient philosophies, which emphasize mindfulness and focused attention as the keys to:

- Personal growth
- Wisdom
- Excellence in all endeavors

Just as Stoicism, Zen Buddhism, and Vedanta teach full presence in every action, deep work applies the same principle to professional and creative success.

The Benefits of Practicing Deep Work

- Clearer Thinking – Eliminating distractions allows for deeper concentration and better problem-solving.
- Higher-Quality Results – Focusing deeply improves the accuracy and creativity of work.
- Greater Efficiency – Tasks get completed faster and with fewer mistakes.

- Reduced Stress – A focused mind experiences less overwhelm and mental exhaustion.
- Increased Fulfillment – Deep work creates a sense of achievement and purpose in one's work.

By practicing deep work regularly, individuals can enhance mental clarity, boost creativity, and achieve success in both their professional and personal lives.

Conclusion: The Power of Focus in a Meaningful Life
To lead a productive and fulfilling life, mastering focus is essential. The blend of ancient wisdom and modern science

highlights the timeless power of focused attention in achieving success and personal growth.

By strengthening concentration, removing distractions, and applying lessons from history's greatest thinkers, individuals can unlock the true potential of focus and experience a remarkable transformation.

The Connection Between Focus and Manifestation

Have you ever considered how focus influences manifestation?

Research suggests that we have around 60,000 thoughts daily, many of which are repetitive. If our minds are cluttered with trivial worries or negativity, we lose the ability to focus on what truly matters.

Imagine your dreams as scattered sunlight. Without focus, they remain diffused and weak. But when you apply focus, like a magnifying glass, all that energy concentrates on one point—bringing your goals to life.

Just as a piece of paper ignites under focused sunlight, your dreams ignite into reality when you direct your mental energy toward them.

- Take Control: Focus Your Mind, Manifest Your Dreams
- Sharpen your focus
- Align your thoughts with your goals
- Direct your energy toward what truly matters

By doing so, you will witness your aspirations materialize before your eyes, turning possibilities into reality.

CHAPTER TWELVE

HARMONY OF EMOTIONS

The Whispering Tree of the Solomon Islands

Deep in the lush, dense jungle of the Solomon Islands, hidden beneath a canopy of towering trees and vibrant plants, stood a tree unlike any other.

Its massive trunk was adorned with ancient carvings, each marking a story from generations long past. The villagers spoke in hushed tones about this tree, sharing legends that had been passed down for centuries.

A Tree That Felt Emotions

Generations ago, the village elders uncovered an extraordinary truth—the sacred tree was deeply connected to the emotions of the villagers. When joy filled the village—when children laughed, families gathered, and celebrations echoed through the land—the tree seemed to rejoice with them.

Its leaves became vibrant, glowing in emerald green, and its presence radiated a gentle warmth under the sunlight—a sign of harmony and unity.

But when sadness, anger, or despair spread through the village, the tree felt their pain. Its once radiant leaves faded into dull browns, becoming dry and brittle. Its branches drooped, lowering toward the ground as if mourning alongside the tribe. The villagers respected and feared this sacred connection, knowing that their own emotions shaped the fate of the tree—and, in turn, the balance of their entire village.

When Discord Wounded the Village Heart

One year, a deep conflict took hold of the tribe. Arguments over resources grew bitter, turning friends into rivals and families against each other. Joyful conversations turned into angry disputes, once-close neighbors avoided eye contact, and the once-carefree laughter of children was replaced by a heavy silence.

The sacred tree bore witness to their pain, and its suffering was undeniable.

Its leaves lost their vibrant green, fading into a lifeless gray. Its branches slumped, no longer reaching toward the sky, and its once mighty presence seemed frail and withered.

The villagers, seeing the tree's sorrow, felt a deep unease. They knew that if the tree was suffering, their village was suffering too. Something had to change.

The tribe gathered in the village center, seeking guidance from their elders. The wise leaders, with years of knowledge, gently reminded them:

"Only unity and forgiveness can heal the wounds you have inflicted—on yourselves and on the sacred tree."

One elder recited a powerful truth:

"For every minute you remain angry, you give up sixty seconds of peace of mind." – Ralph Waldo Emerson

A Gathering for Unity and Healing

Moved by the wisdom of their elders, the villagers decided to hold a great gathering beneath the sacred tree.

That evening, they lit bonfires, their golden flames dancing brightly, illuminating faces that had once turned away in anger.

One by one, villagers began to share their feelings, speaking from the heart.

Apologies were given and accepted.

Old friends embraced, forgiving past grievances.

Families reunited, letting go of resentment.

As the night deepened, the sound of drums echoed gently through the jungle, and songs of unity filled the air, reminding everyone of their shared history and love for one another.

A wave of peace washed over the village, binding their hearts together once more—as though they were beating as one.

The Sacred Tree Revived

With each act of forgiveness and every moment of reconnection, something miraculous began to unfold.

The sacred tree—once withered and sorrowful—began to heal.

Its leaves, once gray and lifeless, slowly regained their rich emerald hue.

Its branches, which had drooped under the weight of despair, rose once more, reaching toward the sunlight with renewed strength—as if celebrating alongside the villagers.

The people watched in awe and gratitude as the tree flourished before their eyes.

At that moment, they realized a profound truth—their emotions shaped their world, not just within their hearts and minds, but in the life around them.

The sacred tree was no longer just a symbol; it was a living testament to the power of unity, love, and emotional balance.

Through this experience, the villagers embraced a new way of living—one where forgiveness, understanding, and harmony became the foundation of their community and happiness.

"Your beliefs become your thoughts, your thoughts become your words, your words become your actions, your actions become your habits, your habits become your values, your values become your destiny." – Mahatma Gandhi

"Unity is strength... when there is teamwork and collaboration, wonderful things can be achieved." – Mattie Stepanek

A Timeless Lesson for Future Generations

The story of the sacred tree became a treasured lesson, passed down from grandparents to grandchildren around evening fires.

The villagers learned to cherish positivity, kindness, and unity, realizing that their emotions had the power to shape reality. They saw that their feelings did not just affect their own lives—they influenced their community, environment, and future generations.

From that day forward, the sacred tree stood tall, no longer just a part of the jungle, but a living reminder of a powerful truth:

- Unity strengthens.
- Love heals.
- Emotions shape the world around us.

The villagers understood that by nurturing compassion, forgiveness, and harmony, they could create a future filled with peace and prosperity.

The sacred tree's story became more than just a legend—it was a guiding light, inspiring all who heard it to live with kindness and wisdom, ensuring that their village flourished for generations to come.

"The strength of a community lies not in its numbers, but in the unity of its hearts." – Mattie Stepanek

The Power of Emotions in Parenting

Lessons from Taare Zameen Par

The movie Taare Zameen Par is a powerful reflection of how a child's emotional and mental well-being is shaped by the way they are treated, especially by parents and teachers.

Aamir Khan's character, Ram Shankar Nikumbh, helps us see the inner struggles of Ishaan, a young boy with dyslexia who experiences the world differently.

Instead of being understood and supported, Ishaan faces:

- Constant scolding
- High expectations
- Harsh comparisons to other children
- The Harm of Negative Parenting Approaches

Ishaan's parents, especially his father, believe that:

- Strict discipline leads to success
- Punishment and criticism will push Ishaan to work harder
- Tough love is necessary for improvement

However, instead of helping him grow, these negative emotions break him down.

He becomes filled with fear and self-doubt.

He starts believing he is not good enough.

He feels like a failure, undeserving of love and acceptance.

This deep emotional impact shows how anger, frustration, and unrealistic expectations can harm a child's confidence and mental health.

Children Absorb What They Are Given

The movie reminds us that children are not born with self-doubt or fear.

These feelings develop when they are repeatedly made to feel incapable or unworthy.

A child who grows up hearing "You are not good enough" starts believing it.

A child who experiences support and encouragement develops confidence and resilience.

The lesson is clear: Parents and teachers play a crucial role in shaping a child's emotional world. The emotions they give to a child will determine how that child sees themselves and their future.

"Children are great imitators, so give them something great to imitate." – Anonymous

Helping Children Grow with Positivity

Children take in everything around them—the words, actions, and feelings of others. The way they are treated, especially by their parents, shapes how they see themselves and the world.

If children grow up in a home filled with love, patience, and support, they become confident and positive. But if they are always criticized, compared, or made to feel unworthy, they may struggle with self-esteem for the rest of their lives.

The Role of Parents in Building Confidence

It is the parents' responsibility to raise their children with kindness and understanding. Instead of focusing on what they lack, parents should encourage their strengths. Instead of forcing them to be like others, they should help them discover their unique talents.

Children who feel loved and accepted will naturally believe in themselves and learn to handle life's ups and downs.

What True Strength Means

Many parents think that being strict and demanding will help their children prepare for life's challenges. But real strength comes from feeling loved and secure.

When children feel safe and valued, they grow up confident, ready to face difficulties, learn from mistakes, and succeed in their way.

Creating the Right Environment for Growth

By giving children a positive and supportive space, parents help them grow emotionally and mentally. Every child is special, and with the right support, they can reach their full potential in their unique way. Parents play a crucial role in a child's brain programming—the belief they put in their child becomes the foundation of that child's self-worth and confidence.

Loving words, encouragement, and patience shape how a child sees themselves and the world.
When parents believe in their child's abilities, the child learns to believe in themselves too.

"The soul is healed by being with children." – Fyodor Dostoevsky

How Childhood Experiences Shape Our Thinking

From birth, children learn from their surroundings. They watch, listen, and absorb what their parents, teachers, and society tell them. These early lessons from childhood programming, shape their thoughts, behaviors, and beliefs about life. This programming affects how they think, what they aim for, and how they see success or failure.

How Childhood Programming Works

1. Childhood Programming Creates Thoughts

A child's brain is like a sponge, taking in everything without questioning it. Whatever they hear repeatedly becomes their truth.

For example:

If a child hears "Money is hard to earn," they will grow up believing that becoming wealthy is difficult.

If a child is told "You are smart," they will develop confidence in their intelligence.

These early messages shape their thoughts, building their view of themselves and the world.

2. Thoughts Create Rules

Once a child believes something, it turns into a rule that guides their actions and decisions.

For example:

A child who hears "You must be perfect to succeed" might grow up afraid of making mistakes.

A child taught "Hard work always pays off" will believe that effort leads to success.

These mental rules shape how they face challenges, make choices, and see success or failure.

3. Rules Create Limitations

Some rules help children grow, but others can hold them back.

For example:

If a child hear "We can't afford that" too often, they may believe that wealth is out of reach, making them settle for less.

If a child is told "You're bad at math", they might avoid jobs that need math skills, even if they could learn with practice.

These limitations are not always real, but because they were taught so early, the child believes them as true.

4. Information Shapes Dreams

The messages children receive shape their goals. Positive words expand their dreams, while negative words limit them.

For example:

A child who hears "You can achieve anything" will aim high and chase big dreams.

A child told "Don't aim too high" may settle for less, thinking success is not for them.

Children's dreams are built not just on their interests, but also on what they are told is possible. A child who is encouraged will grow up believing in opportunities, while a child raised with fear may limit themselves without even realizing it.

The Power of Positive Programming

The good news is that childhood programming is not permanent. Beliefs can be changed.

For example:

Instead of "We can't afford that," parents can say "Let's find a way to make it happen." This teaches a mindset of possibilities instead of scarcity.

Instead of "You're not good at math," saying "You can improve with practice" builds confidence in learning.

Using phrases like "If you work hard, you'll succeed" helps children develop motivation and a strong work ethic.

By replacing negative beliefs with positive ones, anyone can break free from limiting thoughts and build a mindset that leads to success and happiness.

Final Thoughts

Beliefs are not fixed—they are shaped by our early experiences. Some beliefs limit us, while others push us to achieve more. By understanding this, we can change our thinking, set new goals, and live up to our full potential.

"You become what you believe." – Oprah Winfrey

My Story: How My Family's Love Changed Me

Looking back at my journey, I remember one moment that completely changed my mindset.

During my school years, I struggled with bad grades. No matter how much I tried, my marks were disappointing, and I started to believe that I was not good enough.

At home, my parents always believed in me. My mother, in particular, had unshakable faith in my abilities. She would often say, "It's impossible that my son cannot succeed." Her trust in me made me feel both proud and guilty because I knew I was not living up to her expectations.

Then, one day, relatives visited our home. During their conversation, they casually remarked, "We heard his grades are really poor."

As expected, my mother immediately defended me, repeating her usual phrase—"It's impossible." But this time, I saw something different in her eyes. Behind her confidence, I sensed worry and disappointment.

That night, I couldn't sleep. I kept thinking about how much she believed in me, even when I had no faith in myself.

The next day, I made a decision—I would change my mindset and prove her right.

I started studying with full dedication, setting small goals, and improving my study habits. Whenever I felt like giving up, I reminded myself of her words. Slowly, my grades began to improve, and with them, my confidence grew.

How My Parents' Belief Changed Me

If my parents had scolded me or shown disappointment, I might have given up completely. Instead, their unshaken belief in me became my motivation to succeed.

They didn't judge me or make me feel like a failure. Instead, they guided me with love and support, reminding me that I was capable of achieving more.

Had they reacted with anger, I might have remained a struggling student, convinced I could never do better. But because they responded with faith and encouragement, I naturally wanted to improve—not out of pressure, but out of a desire to make them proud.

The Power of Positive Emotions in Our Lives

Emotions shape our thoughts, choices, and actions.

Positive emotions help us grow, connect, and succeed.

Negative emotions, if unchecked, can lead to stress, self-doubt, and poor decisions.

Understanding how emotions work helps us navigate challenges, build strong relationships, and create a life of success and happiness.

That's why it's important to feel as if you have already achieved your goals.

The subconscious mind does not know the difference between reality and imagination—so when you believe in your success, your mind starts working to turn it into reality.

GRATITUDE'S RADIANCE

Introduction

Gratitude is a powerful idea valued in many cultures and religions. It helps people feel more connected to a higher power and brings more peace and happiness into life.

Gratitude isn't just a short feeling—it's a way of thinking that changes how we see the world. Gratitude can improve both our mind and body while bringing us closer to the divine.

What is Gratitude?

Gratitude means noticing and being thankful for the good things in life, whether big or small.

It includes:

- Feeling thankful for help or kindness
- Appreciating simple blessings
- Seeing how everything in life is connected

Gratitude is more than just saying "thank you." It's choosing to focus on what's good, even during hard times.

Gratitude and Spirituality

In many spiritual paths, gratitude is a way to feel closer to the divine.

For example:

In Christianity, people show gratitude through prayer, thanking God for His love and blessings.

In Hinduism, bowing down with respect (pranama) is a way to show thankfulness to the divine in all living things.

Being thankful helps us see the goodness in the world and reminds us we are part of something bigger than ourselves.

PRANAMA

"Gratitude unites faiths through prayer and reverence."

Gratitude in Ancient Spiritual Teachings

Many ancient spiritual beliefs teach that gratitude is a two-way energy—what we give, we receive. When people express gratitude, they connect with the natural flow of abundance, creating a cycle of positive energy.

This idea is also seen in the Law of Attraction, which says that being thankful attracts more good things into life. The more we focus on what we have, the more blessings we receive.

Gratitude as a Source of Hope

In life, hope is like a guiding light, helping people through difficult times. Gratitude shifts attention from what is missing to what is already present. This simple change in focus builds hope, reminding us that even in hard times, there is still something to be thankful for.

When we notice the good in our lives, we start believing that more good things are possible. Gratitude shows us that positive change has already happened, and it can happen again. It gives strength to keep moving forward, even when results are not yet visible.

By focusing on blessings, we stay in a hopeful, high-energy state. This emotional state is key for manifestation—it matches the energy of our desires. The more we feel thankful, the more we attract things to be thankful for. Gratitude turns waiting into trusting and wishing into believing. Practicing gratitude daily helps us stay hopeful, calm, and ready to receive what we are manifesting.

Gratitude Creates a Positive Mindset

When people develop a habit of gratitude, they start noticing the good things in their lives. This helps them stay positive, even when facing difficult situations.

Ancient teachings often show how gratitude and hope are connected:

- Stoic philosophy teaches people to focus on what they can control and to be grateful for challenges, seeing them as chances to grow.
- Buddhism views gratitude as a way to let go of endless desires and find peace in the present, leading to a hopeful and fulfilling life.

By choosing gratitude, people train their minds to see opportunities instead of obstacles, allowing them to move forward with strength and hope. Which helps to reprogram their mind in the positive direction ultimately making their life better.

Simple Ways to Practice Gratitude Every Day

Gratitude is not just a spiritual idea—it is something that can be practiced daily to bring happiness and peace into life. Making gratitude a habit helps shift focus from problems to blessings, creating a more positive mindset.

Easy Ways to Practice Gratitude in Daily Life

Keep a Gratitude Journal

Writing in a gratitude journal each day is a simple but powerful habit. Take a few minutes to write down three things you are thankful for.

This daily practice helps your mind focus on the good, even during hard times.

Say "Thank You" More Often

Take time to thank people—with a smile or simple words. It builds better relationships and creates a positive mood.

Create Simple Gratitude Rituals

Make gratitude part of your routine—like saying thanks before meals. Weekly reflection on what went well builds lasting thankfulness.

With these easy habits, gratitude becomes a way of living, bringing more joy and peace every day.

Ancient Wisdom on Gratitude

Looking at history and different cultures shows how gratitude has always been important for personal growth and spiritual well-being. Many traditions see gratitude as a key to happiness, wisdom, and inner peace.

1. Stoicism (Ancient Greek Philosophy)

The Stoic philosophers of ancient Greece, like Seneca and Marcus Aurelius, believed that gratitude brings peace and emotional strength.

Instead of being grateful for material things, the Stoics believed in appreciating one's ability to face challenges with courage and wisdom.

By focusing on what is within our control, Stoicism teaches us to be thankful for personal growth, self-discipline, and inner strength.

2. Buddhist Teachings on Gratitude

Buddhism connects gratitude with mindfulness, acceptance, and contentment.

By recognizing that everything in life is temporary, people learn to cherish each moment and appreciate what they have.

This awareness helps develop gratitude for life's small joys, leading to a deep sense of peace and happiness.

3. Native American Spirituality

Many Native American traditions treat gratitude as something sacred.

Gratitude ceremonies help people feel connected to nature, each other, and the world.

These rituals teach that sharing and expressing thanks create harmony, unity, and a strong community.

Timeless Lessons on Gratitude

Across different philosophies and traditions, gratitude is seen as a way to find peace, happiness, and connection.

By learning from these ancient teachings, we can apply gratitude in our daily lives, making it a source of strength, peace, and joy.

Health Benefits of Gratitude

Gratitude is not only good for the mind and soul, but it also has proven health benefits. Research shows that practicing gratitude regularly can improve both mental and physical well-being.

1. Better Mental Health
Studies show that people who practice gratitude feel less anxious and depressed.

Focusing on the good things in life instead of negativity helps improve emotional well-being.

2. Lower Stress Levels

Gratitude helps people handle stress better.

When faced with difficult situations, those with a grateful mindset feel more resilient and positive.

3. Improved Sleep Quality

People who express gratitude before bedtime sleep better and longer.

Thinking about positive things before sleeping helps the mind relax, leading to a more restful night.

4. Better Physical Health

Research shows that grateful individuals have:

Lower blood pressure

Stronger immune systems

A reduced risk of heart disease

A positive mindset contributes to better overall health.

Conclusion

Gratitude is a powerful force that connects spiritual, mental, and physical well-being. Its roots in ancient wisdom and its scientific benefits show that it is valuable across all cultures and times.

Gratitude acts as:

- A bridge between people and the divine
- A source of hope during tough times
- A key to mental and physical health

As we navigate modern life, ancient wisdom reminds us that practicing gratitude—through journaling, mindfulness, and expressing thanks—helps us feel happier, healthier, and more at peace.

Gratitude is a simple but powerful habit. When we make it a part of our daily lives, it enriches our experience and makes life more meaningful.

CHAPTER FOURTEEN

UNLEASHING EFFORT

Amit and the Battle Against Procrastination

In the bustling city of Mumbai, among the crowded streets and lively markets, lived a young boy named Amit.

Amit was a dreamer, always lost in his thoughts and ideas. His heart was filled with big dreams, but one habit kept holding him back—procrastination.

A Dreamer Stuck in Delay

Amit spent his days imagining a future full of success and achievements.

He dreamed of doing great things but always said, "I will start tomorrow."

He would sit by the window of his small room, watching the city's endless movement, picturing all the possibilities that awaited him.

But while the city kept moving forward, Amit stayed in the same place, trapped in his habit of postponing tasks.

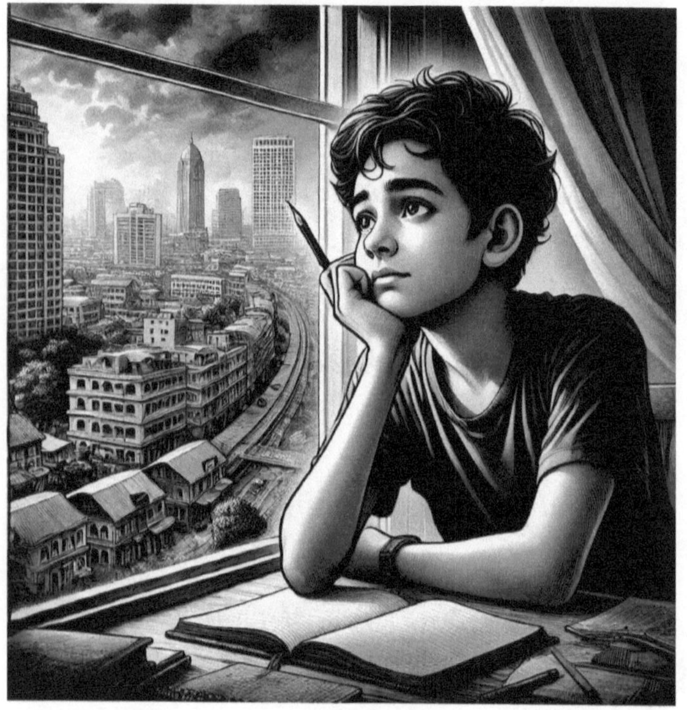

He dreamt of becoming a successful entrepreneur, creating a business empire that would rival the biggest names in the industry. However, his dreams remained confined to the corners of his mind, as he struggled to break free from the chains of procrastination.

His parents, hardworking individuals who had migrated to the city in search of a better life, observed their son's potential fading away. They knew that Amit possessed the intelligence and creativity to achieve great things, but they also knew that mere dreams wouldn't be enough.

One day, as Amit sat lost in thought, his father entered the room with a determined look on his face. He handed Amit a pen and a notebook, urging him to write down his dreams and the steps he needed to take to turn them into reality.

Amit hesitated but complied, sketching out a plan that seemed both ambitious and achievable. However, days turned into weeks, and the notebook gathered dust on the shelf. Amit's parents watched with a heavy heart as their son's dreams languished in the prison of procrastination.

They decided it was time to intervene and help Amit realize the power of action.

Amit's father, a small business owner, took him to his workplace one day. The small manufacturing unit was a stark contrast to the grand visions Amit had for his future.

His father introduced him to the challenges and the rewards of hard work, emphasizing the importance of taking the first step. Inspired by his father's stories and the reality check he desperately needed, Amit decided to confront his procrastination head-on. He revisited the notebook, this time with a newfound determination.

Each day, he set small goals for himself, breaking down his dreams into manageable tasks. The once-idle notebook became a roadmap, guiding him toward his aspirations.

Amit's journey was not without its share of setbacks. There were moments of self-doubt and times when the weight of responsibility seemed overwhelming. However, he refused to let procrastination take control. Instead, he embraced the power of action, learning from his mistakes and persevering through challenges.

As weeks turned into months, Amit transformed. The dreamer who once lived in the realm of possibilities became a doer, fueled by the ray of ambition.

He enrolled in entrepreneurship courses, networked with industry professionals, and even started a small venture of his own. His efforts bore fruit sooner than he expected. Amit's innovative ideas caught the attention of investors, and his business began to flourish.

The boy who was once lost in his thoughts had now emerged as a young entrepreneur, creating waves in the very industry he had dreamt of conquering. Amit's story spread across the city, inspiring others to shed the shackles of procrastination and take charge of their destinies.

His parents, with tears of pride in their eyes, watched as their son's journey unfolded, proving that hard work and action could indeed turn dreams into reality. In the heart of Mumbai, where dreams often collide with the harsh realities of life, Amit stood as a testament to the transformative power of determination and action.

The boy who once believed in the magic of thoughts alone had learned that it was the alchemy of hard work and perseverance that could turn dreams into gold. In the intricate web of life, much like the tale of Amit, our journey is an intricate dance of actions and aspirations.

Throughout this narrative, I've delved into the realms of manifestation, unraveling the power of thoughts and the subconscious in molding our dreams into reality. Yet, let's not be deceived; these methods are but whispers in the wind without the pivotal ingredient: action. Sitting in silent meditation won't bestow upon you everything you desire.

Manifestation techniques serve as guides, unveiling opportunities, ideas, and stepping stones to your goals. They lay out a roadmap, akin to a GPS, directing you to shorter paths and warning of potential obstacles.

However, the onus is on you to take the steps and traverse the route. The subconscious mind illuminates the way, but it is your toil that transforms dreams into tangible achievements.

Remember, you must become capable for dreams to materialize.

Consider this: You wish to elevate your monthly income from $20,000 to $100,000 in a year. But for the next year, you do not make any specific changes in your actions, or habits. You do not take any step towards achieving your goals so, just think how will the universe know whether you are worthy of the dream or not. Because once you have dreamt, it's not a mere wish anymore; it's a goal. Now, draft a plan. What technologies or skills do you need to acquire? Break it down into manageable steps.

Perhaps five technologies in a year; that's your target. Plan quarterly or monthly. Allocate time, like "two months for one technology." Calculate the daily commitment needed. This structured approach is the catalyst.

Now, trust the process. Initiate action. Let your subconscious transform your hard work into smart work, propelling you toward your goal effortlessly. Imagine you're among a hundred applicants for a job.

Your subconscious places you in the top ten, influencing the interviewer in ways you can't fathom. Let me illustrate with my story.

My story

In 2018, I worked at a call center in Gurugram and was happy with my job. Then, a company named ABC offered me a job with a small salary, but it involved manual work laying internet cables. My current job felt much better.

I told my sister, Swati, about it, and she scolded me. She thought I was wasting my potential. Her words made me angry, and I decided to prove her wrong.

I started studying at night while working during the day. On weekends, I practiced in labs to improve my skills.

By April 2019, I applied for a job at XYZ with a friend's help. I studied hard and barely slept, but it paid off.

Even though I answered only 20% of the questions correctly in my first interview, I still moved to the next round and eventually got the job with a good salary increase.

My sister was shocked. I wasn't the best at technical skills, but the company still kept me.

A friend who also applied for the job told me, "You're lucky. You'll learn a lot here. But it's strange—you only had to answer 20% right, while I had to get 80% and go through six interviews to get hired."

Even after a year, I still didn't understand many technical terms. One day, my boss said he was surprised I had lasted so long because people with little knowledge usually get fired in a few months.

That's when I realized my success wasn't just because of my skills. It was my determination and the power of manifestation. A few years ago, XYZ was on my vision board.

The universe helped me achieve my goal.

Just like a doctor treats a wound, it is the universe that heals. My hard work opened the door, but the universe made sure I walked through it.

Epilogue

I would like to thank you for being a part of this transformative journey through the pages of our exploration, I hope that you have understood the intricate dance between the universe and human beings, delving into the profound connection that binds us with the universe.

As we navigate the realms of the subconscious and conscious mind and how these both affect our reality, it unfolds like a tapestry woven with the threads of self-awareness and the underlying forces that shape our reality.

At the heart of this odyssey is the exploration of the Law of Attraction, a magnetic force that draws parallel lines between our thoughts and the cosmic energies around us.

The book serves as a guide, illuminating the path to understanding how our thoughts, whether consciously or subconsciously crafted, mold the universe's response to our desires.

It urges readers to become architects of their destinies, understanding that the mind is a powerful tool that shapes the reality we experience.

A pivotal chapter is dedicated to the art of manifestation and affirmations, unlocking the secrets to consciously shaping our reality. Through the careful crafting of intentions and the repetition of positive affirmations, the reader is invited to witness the alchemical process of turning dreams into reality.

The book underscores the importance of aligning thoughts, emotions, and actions with the desired outcomes, creating a harmonious resonance that resonates with the universe's vibrations.

One of the book's standout techniques is the power of visualization as a manifestation tool. Through vivid imagery and sensory exploration, readers are encouraged to paint mental pictures of their desired outcomes.

The narrative unfolds as a guide through the labyrinth of the mind, illustrating how visualization serves as a bridge between the conscious and subconscious realms, paving the way for the manifestation of dreams into tangible reality.

However, the journey is not without its challenges. The book tackles the formidable task of combating negative beliefs entrenched in the recesses of the mind. It serves as a beacon, illuminating the dark corners of self-doubt and negativity.

Readers are equipped with tools to dismantle these mental barriers, replacing them with positive beliefs that act as catalysts for transformative change. The narrative becomes a rallying cry for self-empowerment, urging individuals to reclaim control over their thoughts and beliefs.

A significant portion of the book is devoted to the arduous yet rewarding process of reprogramming the mind for positive beliefs. It dissects the mechanisms through which the mind absorbs and internalizes beliefs, offering insights into the subconscious programming that often dictates our actions.

Armed with knowledge, readers embark on a journey of self-discovery, dismantling limiting beliefs and constructing a mental framework that supports their aspirations.

The book also pays homage to the symbiotic relationship between the power of hard work and the art of manifestation. It dispels the notion that manifestation is a passive process, emphasizing the importance of coupling intention with action.

Through real-life anecdotes and practical guidance, readers are inspired to roll up their sleeves and actively participate in the co-creation of their destinies.

The narrative celebrates the fusion of intention and effort, showcasing the dynamic synergy that propels individuals toward their goals.

In conclusion, the book orchestrates a symphony of interconnected themes, weaving together the cosmic dance between the universe and human beings. It invites readers to a profound exploration of the subconscious and conscious mind, unraveling the mysteries that shape our perceptions and experiences.

Through the lens of the Law of Attraction, the narrative becomes a compass, guiding individuals toward the manifestation of their desires.

The journey is illuminated by the transformative power of manifestation and affirmations, supported by the potent technique of visualization. Yet, the path is not without its hurdles, as the book tackles the formidable task of dismantling negative beliefs and reprogramming the mind for positivity.

Finally, the narrative underscores the dynamic interplay between hard work and the art of manifestation, emphasizing that the alchemy of success requires both intention and action. As readers traverse these pages, they are not only armed with knowledge but also equipped with the tools to actively shape their destinies and dance in harmony with the universe.